GREAT AMERICAN

FOR
JAMES BEARD
AND JULIA CHILD,
WHO LIT THE LAMP
AND SHOWED US
THE WAY

COOKING SCHOOLS

GREAT AMERICAN COOKING SCHOOLS

American Food & California Wine
Bountiful Bread: Basics to Brioches
Christmas Feasts from History
Romantic & Classic Cakes
Cooking of the South
Dim Sum & Chinese One-Dish Meals
Fine Fresh Food—Fast
Fresh Garden Vegetables
Ice Cream & Ices
Omelettes & Soufflés
Pasta! Cooking It, Loving It
Quiche & Pâté
Soups & Salads
Successful Parties: Simple & Elegant

BOUNTIFUL BREAD
BASICS TO BRIOCHES

LYNN KUTNER

ILLUSTRATED BY MACEO MITCHELL

IRENA CHALMERS COOKBOOKS, INC. • **NEW YORK**

*To my darling husband Richard, without whose ability
to type and to taste there would be no book.*

IRENA CHALMERS COOKBOOKS, INC.

PUBLISHER
Irena Chalmers

Sales and Marketing Director
Diane J. Kidd

Managing Editor
Jean Atcheson

Series Design
Helene Berinsky

Cover Design
Milton Glaser
Karen Skelton, *Associate Designer*

Cover Photography
Matthew Klein

Editor for this book
Barbara Spiegel

Typesetting
Acu-Type, Inc., Clinton, CT

Printing
Lucas Litho, Inc., Baltimore, MD

Editorial Offices
23 East 92nd Street
New York, NY 10028
(212) 289-3105

Sales Offices
P.O. Box 322
Brown Summit, NC 27214
(919) 656-3115

ISBN # 0-941034-03-8
© 1982 by Lynn Kutner. All rights reserved.
Printed and published in the United States of America
by Irena Chalmers Cookbooks, Inc.

LIBRARY OF CONGRESS
CATALOG CARD NO.: 81-68840
    Kutner, Lynn
        Bountiful bread: Basics to brioches.

Greensboro, NC: Chalmers, Irena Cookbooks, Inc.
84 p.
8108   810722

ABCDE65432   695/4

Contents

Introduction

Working with yeast dough is an immensely satisfying experience. Not only are you creating a dough that is actually alive and growing in front of you, but you are working directly with your hands when kneading and shaping the dough. There is no other experience in cooking where you become so closely involved with your creation; no implement or tool need come between you and the dough.

Once you understand the properties of yeast, the effect of other ingredients on it, and basic baking techniques, the possible variations will seem limitless. To avoid cluttering the book with endless advice on these subjects, the General Information section will discuss them in detail, and the first recipe in the Basic Bread section (White Bread) as well as the first recipe in the Advanced Techniques section (Brioche) will take you step by step through the entire yeast dough process. After that, the recipes will be written in a more concise, compact manner. I strongly recommend that you read carefully through the section that follows and actually prepare at least one batch of white bread and one batch of brioche before you head toward the more complicated breads and cakes.

General Information

WHAT YEAST IS

Yeast is a living plant; it is a fungus, a parasite that must ingest other organic matter in order to subsist. The preferred food of yeast happens to be gluten, the protein component of wheat flour. It actually feeds upon the gluten, multiplies, and produces carbon dioxide and alcohol as by-products. The carbon dioxide bubbles cause the bread to rise, and if you allow the dough to over-rise, the alcohol will sour the dough; it will actually taste like bad whiskey.

Two Kinds of Yeast

Yeast is available commercially in two forms — dry, powdered yeast and fresh cake yeast. The powdered yeast has been made dormant by a sort of freeze-drying process and is theoretically awakened when it is dissolved in water. Cake yeast is actually awake and functioning in the cake form. In fact, the cake consists of yeast cells and cereal starch upon which the cell's feed until you mix it into a dough so that it can feed upon gluten. I prefer cake yeast because I believe it produces a bread of slightly greater volume, and if I need to retard the rising action of a dough, it will revive more readily when exposed to warmth. If you cannot find a source for fresh yeast, do not despair — all the recipes include instructions for the use of dry yeast. If the dry yeast "proofs" well (see below), you will obtain fine results.

Proofing the Yeast

Occasionally, a package of dry yeast will be dead, even though the date indicates that it should be fresh and lively for the next eight months or so. To avoid the frustration of making up a whole batch of dough, and having it refuse to rise, test your dry yeast before adding it to the other ingredients. To do this, simply dissolve the yeast in a quarter cup of cool water and add a half teaspoon of sugar to it. If the mixture starts foaming and bubbling within five minutes, it is good. Add the whole foaming mass to the other ingredients. You may, of course, proof fresh yeast, but I have never found this necessary. If the cake of fresh yeast looks and feels good, it is good. Fresh yeast should be an even, creamy tan color with a smooth, dry texture. Any dark brown spots may be gently shaved off with a knife. If the cake has become moldy, it should be discarded.

FLOUR

The only kind of white flour used for the recipes in this book is an unbleached, all-purpose flour. Its gluten content is relatively high, compared to the other flours on the supermarket shelf, which makes it fine for yeast doughs. It is called all-purpose because it consists of a mixture of two different kinds of wheat: hard wheat, which has a high gluten content, and soft wheat, which has little gluten (cake flour).

For the whole-grain breads, it is preferable to use stone-ground whole-grain flours, rather than those that are commercially ground, on a large scale, with steel. Stone grinding is done at a much cooler temperature than steel grinding, and a great deal more of the grain's nutrients are preserved. Whole-grain flours are milled from the entire grain: the bran, the germ, and the endosperm (white part) combined. The germ, which is especially rich in vitamins and minerals, becomes rancid quickly. Because of this, all whole-grain flours (whole wheat, whole rye, cornmeal, buckwheat, etc.) should be refrigerated as soon as possible. If you have a large freezer, they may be kept there. You should always try to buy whole-grain flours at a store that sells them in quantity, so that you know that they are fresh.

In addition to flour, other ingredients have an effect on the functioning of yeast in a dough. Ingredients which add richness, such as butter, egg yolks, whole eggs, milk, cream, sour cream, sugar, honey, and molasses, tend to slow down the action of the yeast. Salt also acts as a yeast inhibitor, to some extent; if you make a salt-free dough, it will rise much faster than usual.

POTATOES

I have just listed ingredients that somewhat retard yeast's function. There is a very surprising one that can help the yeast and the entire dough as well: hot mashed potatoes. The starch in potatoes helps to feed the yeast and causes the cells to multiply faster. However, by far the most interesting property of potatoes in a yeast dough is their action as a natural preservative. The moisture present in a potato is transferred to the dough and the baked product remains soft and fresh for days without refrigeration (provided the bread or cake is properly wrapped in foil or plastic). The texture of a yeast bread or cake containing potatoes is also somewhat fluffier than that of one made without them, and there is not the slightest trace of a potato taste in the finished product. Most of the recipes in this book contain potatoes, but they are an optional ingredient. If you choose to omit them, you may do so without any other adjustment to the recipe; all the other proportions remain the same.

Note:

Potatoes will keep bread fresh, but they are not a mold inhibitor as is calcium propionate, the artificial preservative that is used commercially.

EQUIPMENT

The amount of paraphernalia required to bake yeast doughs is minimal. As far as the basic preparation of the dough is concerned, you will need only:

1. A large mixing bowl
2. Measuring spoons and cups
3. A large wooden spoon
4. A rubber spatula
5. A large wire whisk (optional)
6. A cloth on which to knead (an old pillow-case, a clean cloth diaper, a flat-textured dish towel — not terrycloth, etc.). I prefer to knead dough on a floured cloth because there is no sticking problem. You tape the cloth to the table, rub some flour into it, and the weave of the fabric will absorb the flour.
7. Masking tape to hold the cloth down. Be sure to tape down the cloth before flouring, or the tape will not stick.
8. A rolling pin, preferably without handles, so that the pressure you exert goes to that part of the dough which you choose to roll out. If you hold onto handles, the application of pressure is out of your control; it is not directly underneath your hand.
9. A few cookie sheets or jelly-roll pans and a couple of loaf pans will take you a long way. The optional pans you may want to acquire are:

> brioche molds (large size and individual roll size)
> savarin mold
> baba molds
> 10-inch angel-food cake pan (tube cake pan)
> Bundt Kuchen or Kugelhupf mold

Glossary of Techniques

1. *Dissolving and Proofing Yeast*

Complete instructions for proofing yeast are on page 8. There is one more point about dissolving the yeast that deserves mention here. Be sure that the water in which you dissolve the yeast is rather cool — about 85 degrees Fahrenheit. One of the major reasons for yeast bread failures is that the yeast is actually killed by being dissolved in water that is too warm. Traditionally, recipes will tell you to dissolve the yeast in lukewarm water, but some people have a rather "hot" idea about lukewarm. Temperatures above 100 degrees are dangerous; some yeasts will survive higher temperatures, but many will die at 100 degrees. There is no harm done in dissolving yeast in cool water. It may take a few moments longer to dissolve, but there are no other consequences.

2. *Prekneading*

This is the process by which you will make the very soft dough on your floured pastry cloth ready to be kneaded. Many of the doughs in my recipes are in a rather soft state when you are told to turn them out of the mixing bowl and onto the cloth. (Some exceptions are pumpernickel, rye, bagels, and cinnamon-raisin-oatmeal-whole wheat doughs, which are heavier and stiffer.) Do not dig in yet or try to knead heartily; you will get stuck in the dough.

Each recipe provides an allotment of flour for prekneading and kneading. Use the prescribed amount to flour the cloth, the dough, and your hands. Gently push the dough toward its center by lifting the edges with the sides of your hands and flipping them inward. Have a small, sharp knife nearby, and if some dough sticks to your hands, scrape it back into the mass quickly, flouring your hands and the dough surface as necessary. Occasionally flip over the whole dough mass. After two or three minutes, the dough will begin to firm up, and you may start vigorous kneading.

3. *Kneading*

First and foremost, do not use your fingertips or fingers. Kneading is properly done using the heel of the hand and the underside of the wrist. This way you will not get stuck in the dough.

Use the allotment of flour to powder the cloth each time the dough seems to be getting sticky. Turn the dough around on the floured cloth to lightly powder its surface. To knead, push and stretch the dough from the center outwards, using the heels of your hands; flip the dough in half and quickly flip the whole mass over. Repeat this process for about five minutes, flouring the cloth as necessary, then rolling the dough around on the floured cloth. Push and stretch, flip in half, turn it over. Use strong, weighty, but quick strokes. When the dough is well kneaded, it will spring back when pressed with a finger.

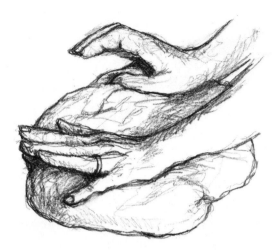

When you push and stretch the dough, you will be creating sticky spots; do not flour them and do not put your hands into them. This is the reason I ask you to flip the dough in half; you, in effect, hide these spots. To avoid adding too much flour, which results in a heavy bread, flour the cloth and not the dough. Then you can roll the dough around on the floured cloth. With this method, you will use much less flour than if you flour the dough directly.

4. *Rising the Dough*

To make really fine-textured yeast breads and cakes, let the dough rise three times. Many recipes call for only two rises, but the finished product does not have nearly as nice a grain.

FIRST RISE: After kneading the dough, place it to rise in a lightly oiled large bowl. Turn the dough over in the bowl to lightly oil its surface. This keeps the dough from drying out as it rises. For breads that should have a thick, crunchy crust (such as pumpernickel, rye, French or Italian loaves, bagels, pizza, and hard rolls), do not oil the rising bowl, as this softens the crust. Simply flour the bowl and cover the dough with a damp cloth. Make sure that the cloth does not dry out. You can put a sheet of plastic wrap loosely over the cloth to help prevent evaporation.)

SECOND RISE: Punch the dough down and turn it out onto the kneading cloth. Knead the dough for about three to five minutes. Replace it in the bowl (re-oiling or reflouring it, if necessary), cover the bowl with the slightly damp cloth, and allow the dough to rise again until almost doubled in size.

THIRD (LAST) RISE: This last rise is the dramatic one. After the second rise, you punch down the dough again, but then shape it and place it in the prepared baking pans. The dough rises in its finished shape for the third rise, and then it is baked. For most recipes, you let the dough triple in size for this third and final rise. Try to remember what the shaped dough looks like when you put it in your pans. Then estimate what triple will look like. One word of advice: you should be satisfied with the size and shape of your bread before you place it in the oven. Do not count on rising taking place in the oven; whatever is gained in the oven will probably be lost in shrinkage as the bread cools.

5. *Preparing Baking Pans*

Thoroughly grease the baking pans with a solid

vegetable shortening. Then lightly flour the pans by sprinkling one to two tablespoons of flour on each greased pan and knocking the flour around until a thin film coats them evenly. Knock out the excess onto the pastry cloth.

6. *Glazing Risen Dough*

In most of the recipes in this book, the doughs are brushed with a whole egg glaze, an egg-white glaze, or butter just before baking. The whole egg glaze consists of an egg beaten with two tablespoons of water. The egg-white glaze consists of one egg white beaten with two tablespoons of water. The whole egg will give the bread (e.g., brioche) a beautiful deep brown gloss when baked. The egg white gives the bread a gloss without darkening it (e.g., rye bread). Melted butter, brushed on breads such as babka and kuchen, gives the finished product an extra rich taste. A pastry brush is useful for applying the glaze.

7. *Placing in the Oven*

Doughs that are placed high in the oven get their tops browned first. Doughs placed low in the oven get their bottoms browned first. Here are some general rules to follow about oven placement:
- Small items, such as rolls, cookies, and biscuits, are baked high in the oven.
- Large items, such as yeast breads and pies, are baked low in the oven.
- Medium-sized items, such as cakes, are baked in the middle of the oven.
- Never bake on the oven floor.

When you are having trouble with baked goods browning too quickly or too slowly, it may help to change the oven level as well as the oven temperature as follows:
- If tops are browning before dough is finished baking — lower the baking level and lower the oven temperature 25 to 50 degrees, and/or lay a piece of foil lightly over the dough.
- If the dough finishes baking but is not browning — raise the baking level and/or raise the oven temperature 25 to 50 degrees.

8. *Baking Time*

A yeast bread or cake that is made with 2½ cups of flour will usually bake in 30 to 35 minutes in a loaf pan or a tube pan. Its width is relatively narrow compared to the same amount of dough baked in a large brioche mold. A large brioche is rather fat through the middle and takes about 45 minutes to bake. There are two ways to test a yeast bread for doneness. The first is that it will sound hollow when tapped, and the second is that a toothpick inserted into the fattest part of the bread will come out absolutely bone dry when the bread is done. (Beware: If a babka is filled with chocolate, butter, sugar, etc., the toothpick may look wet from the filling. Be careful to distinguish between wet filling ingredients and crumbs of dough when examining the toothpick.) The toothpick test is probably the more accurate; I recommend it.

Rolls (small brioches, croissants, etc.) take between 15 and 20 minutes to bake. Because rolls are small, and there is little volume to account for, one can say that a roll is done when it looks done.

When you bake breads and cakes in unusual shapes and sizes of your own invention, there can be no specific baking times given, but there are a few precautions that you can take. If the bread is a very large one, bake it at a relatively slow temperature (325 degrees) to allow the inside to cook before the outside browns. You may also want to cover it lightly with foil even before it becomes very brown; this also will allow the center to cook. As soon as you think it might be finished, test with a toothpick in its fattest part, every five to eight minutes.

9. *Unmolding Breads from Pans*

Non-yeast breads and cakes may be allowed to cool in their baking pans if desired. Not so with yeast breads and cakes. They must be unmolded immediately or they will become terribly soggy. Yeast breads and cakes should slide right out of their pans, if the pans have been properly greased and floured. Leave them on wire racks until cool.

If there is a spot that is sticking, use a small, sharp knife to free the bread. Sometimes some egg glaze will drip into the pan and cause the bread to stick. With a fluted large brioche, where there are many opportunities for the egg glaze to get into the flutes, it is a good idea to make sure that each flute can come free by going quickly and carefully around the flutes with a sharp knife. Do not puncture the bread; run the knife down the flute, touching the metal pan. Then carefully ease the bread out.

10. *Cooling Yeast Breads and Cakes*

With the exception of small roll-sized products (small brioches, croissants, etc.), all yeast doughs should be thoroughly cooled on wire racks before eating. This is because when a yeast product comes hot from the oven, it is heavy with moisture that must evaporate. The hot bread actually weighs more than the cooled bread. This is why you will get indigestion from eating fresh, hot bread — wet, heavy dough will be lying in your stomach. Rolls have such small volume that their excess moisture evaporates quite fast. Therefore, you can eat small brioches and croissants after only a few minutes' cooling. When you eat hot bread in a restaurant, it is always reheated bread, not bread that was never cooled first.

11. *Storing and Freezing*

After breads and cakes have completely cooled on wire racks (three hours for large breads and babkas), wrap them in plastic bags or aluminum foil. For consumption within a few days, leave them at room temperature. (There is an exception: croissants and Danish should be wrapped and refrigerated. Before eating, reheat for eight to ten minutes in a 325-degree oven.) If you want to freeze your breads, place them in the freezer on a tray, unwrapped. After one to two hours, when they are frozen, wrap them carefully in plastic or foil and replace them quickly in the freezer. This way no condensation will form inside the wrapping. Defrost large breads and cakes overnight in the refrigerator with their wrappings opened. Small rolls, croissants, and Danish may be directly reheated in the oven from their frozen state; they do not need defrosting.

Slowing Up a Yeast Dough

If you would like to bake yeast breads and cakes often, but cannot devote eight continuous hours of precious time to your dough, take heart. There is a marvelous solution: slowing up the dough. By reducing the rising action of the dough to a virtual snail's pace, you will never have to devote more than a few minutes' time to the dough for each day that you keep it. You may keep the dough refrigerated for up to three days before baking, or, for longer storage, you may actually freeze it. Here are the detailed instructions on how to slow up a yeast dough.

1. Mix the dough ingredients as usual, but use only half the amount of yeast called for in the recipe (no other proportion changes). Knead the dough as usual. Prepare the dough for the first rise. (Place the dough in an oiled bowl, turn it around in the bowl to lightly oil its surface, and cover with a slightly damp dish towel. Do not oil the bowl for crusty breads, such as rye, pumpernickel, or French bread. Oil would ruin the crust. Simply flour the bowl and cover it with a damp dish towel.)

2. *The three- to four-hour chill:* Now, instead of allowing the dough to rise at room temperature, place it in the refrigerator. You must take into account the richness of your dough to determine how long it will take for a slight rise in the refrigerator. The very rich doughs in the Advanced Techniques section will take three to four hours before there is any perceptible rising. The non-rich doughs (white, whole wheat, pumpernickel, rye, bagels, pizza, French bread, etc.) will take only one and a half to two hours before you will see any rising. At any rate, you want to punch down the dough before it doubles, and then replace it in the refrigerator or freezer. This means that the rich doughs can be left alone to chill for three or four hours, but that the non-rich doughs will have to be punched down two or three times during this initial chilling process so that they do not over-rise.

3. At the end of this three- or four-hour period, the dough should be thoroughly chilled. Take the dough out of the refrigerator and punch it down well. Using your fist, first deflate the center of the dough, then punch around the circumference. Pick the dough up and turn it over. Beat on it a minute or two longer, to be sure that every bit of air has been released from the dough. (This is actually carbon dioxide gas, a product of yeast fermentation, which must be released so that the dough does not sour.) Return the dough to its bowl (re-oil or re-flour if necessary), turn the dough in the bowl if oiled, cover with a slightly damp towel, and refrigerate again. The dough should not have been out of the refrigerator for more than three minutes.

4. Now that the dough is chilled and deflated, its rising action is even slower than before. You may now leave it unattended in the refrigerator for eight hours or so at a time, which means that you can go to work, go to sleep, or just do something else. It does still need punching every time it starts

to rise visibly; about three times in a 24-hour period. Never let the dough double while in storage. You may keep the dough refrigerated for about three days before baking.

5. *Freezing instructions:* For a freezing period of up to one week, you may use either fresh or dry yeast in your dough; for a freezing period of up to one month, you must use fresh yeast. (Dry yeast is not quite as strong as fresh and usually cannot withstand too long a period of freezing.)

After the initial three- to four-hour rise in the refrigerator and the thorough punching down, divide the dough into useful-sized portions (e.g., enough dough for one large brioche or a babka). Place each in a roomy and well-floured plastic bag. Tie the bags at the top; this will leave plenty of air space for the small bit of rising that takes place before the dough becomes solidly frozen. Place the bags of dough in the freezer. When the dough is solidly frozen, you should replace the ties to pack the dough airtight. At this point, it is a good idea to double-bag the dough, to cut down on freezer burn. Date and label the bags. Dough may be safely frozen for one month.

Waking, Shaping and Rising the Slowed or Frozen Dough

The dough is ready to be shaped and allowed its third or final rise at the time of your choosing. Just remember that the final rise will take many hours because of the small amount of yeast used. A non-rich dough made completely or mostly with white flour (white bread, French bread, bagels, etc.) will rise more quickly and needs more watching in this final rise. If you allow a bread to rise more than triple its bulk, it will collapse. It will take at least twice as long to rise as the same dough made with the full amount of yeast, and probably longer, since the dough is cold. See individual recipes for the time given for the full amount of yeast; double the time and you have the minimum amount required for a slowed third rise.

During this final rise, the dough should triple in bulk. Remember, it is not how long you allow your dough to rise that is of final importance; it is how large your dough becomes that is of interest. Time is used only as a guide. If at the end of four hours your dough has not quite tripled, allow it to rise a while longer. Whole-grain doughs (pumpernickel, whole wheat, etc.) will not triple in bulk; they will only double because of the heaviness of the grain. Do not bake your yeast bread or cake unless you are totally satisfied with its size before baking.

Thaw frozen dough slowly in the refrigerator. Readjust the ties on the bags to allow for the rising that will take place during the thaw; otherwise, the dough will tear through the bag. Thawing will take overnight or all day, depending on your time schedule. Now simply treat this dough as if it had merely been slowed in the refrigerator.

Choose one of the following methods for shaping and rising your slowed dough. (When you become adept at making a slow dough, you will find yourself combining these methods to fit your time schedule even better.)

1. Shape the dough and place it in the pan as the individual recipe instructs, and cover the pan with a slightly damp towel. Place a piece of plastic wrap lightly over the towel to keep the towel from drying out during this very long rise. Allow the dough to rise at room temperature until tripled in bulk. Remember that whole-grain doughs only double. Rolls will rise in about half as much time as large shapes. If your room is very cool (60 degrees on a winter's night), rising may take longer.

2. Shape the dough and place it in the pan, as the individual recipe instructs, and cover the pan with a slightly damp towel. Replace in the refrigerator. This rise will be very slow: overnight plus about two to three additional hours at room temperature for large shapes, and about one to two additional hours for rolls.

3. Allow the dough to warm at room temperature before shaping. Then shape and place the

dough in the pan as the recipe instructs. Cover the pan with a slightly damp towel. This fairly warm dough will rise faster than chilled dough, but remember that you have just spent several hours warming up the dough. Allow the dough to triple in size. (Whole-grain doughs only double.)

Glazing and Baking

When the dough has completed its rising in its shape, it is ready for glazing and baking, as the recipe instructs. There is one matter that you must take care of: when a yeast dough is allowed to rise very slowly, it tends to develop many large air bubbles on the surface; these must be broken before baking, or they will swell into big hollow blisters in the oven. Flour a small pair of scissors or a toothpick and burst them. These blisters will become very obvious when you glaze the surface of your risen dough with a brush, so you cannot miss them. These are only surface bubbles; do not worry about the interior of your dough.

Accounting for the Three Rises

The initial three- or four-hour rise in the refrigerator is the first rise. For a refrigerated dough, the second rise consists of the rest of the time that you keep the dough in storage, before taking it out to shape. This is the two- or three-day period in which you punch the dough three times in every 24 hours. The dough, in fact, has had many little rises. All these little rises together will be considered the second rise. For a frozen dough, its overnight thaw in the refrigerator will be considered the second rise. The yeast begins to work slowly, as soon as the thawing begins. The third rise is the same as for a non-slowed dough: the dough is shaped, placed in its pans, and allowed to rise until tripled in bulk (doubled for whole-grain breads).

HANDLING SLOWED DOUGH IN CERTAIN INSTANCES

1. *Freezing Dough with the Full Amount of Yeast*

You can freeze dough that contains the full amount of yeast if you are very careful not to allow the dough to rise more than double in the initial rise. That means that the first rise will take about one hour. Do not forget about it, or it will sour. Then it must be well punched and immediately put in floured bags for freezing. Be sure to leave plenty of air space in which this very active dough can rise, before it becomes solidly frozen. If you do not, the growing dough will burst right through the bags. When the dough is solidly frozen, close the bags airtight.

After this dough has thawed, its final rise in its shape will be twice as fast as that of the dough that has been frozen or slowed with half the amount of yeast. Take this into account when you are about to prepare dough for the freezer. Label your bags of frozen dough carefully as to the amount of yeast used (full amount or half) so that you can approximate the final rising time.

2. *Thawed Dough for Croissants, Danish, and Pizza*

If you are going to turn a batch of frozen dough into croissants, or a crust for pizza, or into anything that requires that it be rolled out into a large area, knead the dough well after thawing. Then place it in an oiled or floured bowl, cover with a damp towel, and let it rest in the refrigerator from two to four hours. Do not knead it again. Simply knock it out of the bowl onto your floured cloth and roll it out with a rolling pin. Proceed with the recipe. Unrested dough will be nearly impossible to roll out.

3. *Slowed Dough for Croissants and Danish*

If you are slowing a batch of dough to make croissants or Danish, do not halve the yeast. The amount of yeast has already been reduced for these recipes. This is because the dough must be chilled and made fairly inactive in order to roll the butter in properly.

THREE HYPOTHETICAL TIMETABLES
FOR PRODUCING BREAD AND CAKE FOR A SATURDAY BRUNCH
(Baked Fresh That Morning)

	Using one-half the yeast and refrigerating for 2 to 3 days	*Using one-half the yeast and freezing*	*Using full amount of yeast and freezing*
Preparing basic dough *(time will depend on your speed and skill)*	40 minutes to 1 hour. Come home from work and prepare from 6 to 7 on Wednesday or Thursday evening.	40 minutes to 1 hour. Prepare from 10 to 11 a.m. on a rainy Saturday morning up to 4 weeks before your party.	40 minutes to 1 hour. Prepare one evening between 8 and 9 p.m. up to 4 weeks before your party.
1st rise and punch down *(dough rises visibly but is not allowed to double)*	About 3 to 4 hours in refrigerator. Will take from 7 to 10 or 11 p.m. Punch down (3 minutes). Go to sleep!	About 3 to 4 hours in refrigerator. Will take from 11 a.m. to 2 or 3 p.m. (Go out to lunch or shopping.) Punch down (3 minutes). Freeze.	About 1 hour in refrigerator or room temperature. Will take from 10 to 11 p.m. Do not forget it! Punch down (3 minutes). Freeze.
2nd rise or rises	About 8 hours. Wake up in the morning and punch down. Replace in refrigerator. Go to work! Punch when you come home and 3 times in every 24 hours.	Thaw in refrigerator starting Friday morning before your brunch.	1. Thaw in refrigerator during the day on Friday if you are to shape on that night. 2. Thaw in refrigerator over Friday night if you want to get up early Saturday morning.
3rd rise *(dough is filled, shaped, placed in prepared pans and allowed to triple in size)*	Shape dough and place in pans Friday evening. Let stand at room temperature 1 or 2 hours to start rising. Refrigerate overnight. Take out in morning and allow rising to continue at room temperature 1 or 2 hours or until complete.		1. Shape late Friday evening. Let rise in refrigerator overnight and then 1 to 2 hours at room temperature Saturday morning. 2. Get up early (7 a.m.) Saturday. Shape and let rise at room temperature for 2 to 3 hours. Less time for rolls.

	Using one-half the yeast and refrigerating for 2 to 3 days	Using one-half the yeast and freezing	Using full amount of yeast and freezing
Baking and glazing	Saturday morning glaze and burst blisters after rise is complete. Bake around 9 or 10 a.m.		Later Saturday morning (somewhere between 9:30 to 10:30) glaze, burst blisters, and bake.
Cooling and eating	Large loaves and cakes should cool 2 to 3 hours.* Eating by 12 or 1 p.m.		Cool 2 to 3 hours. Eat by 12:30 or 1:30. (Rolls need only 10 minutes' cooling.)

*Let rolls rise in refrigerator overnight, and then for about 1 to 2 hours at room temperature. Remember, rolls need only about 10 minutes' cooling — they may be eaten warm.

RECIPES

BASIC BREADS

Wheat is the grain that has the highest gluten content. A grain of wheat consists of three basic parts:

the outer bran coating

the glutenous white part

the wheat germ.

It is only the white part that contains the protein, gluten. Yeast reacts with the gluten in flour, and the dough rises. A bread made completely with white flour will rise higher than one made with the whole wheat grain, because the bran and the germ do not react with the yeast. They are heavy, although healthy, additions to the bread. There are two other grains that contain gluten: they are rye and buckwheat. Rye gluten reacts with the yeast so that the dough increases in bulk, but rye gluten does not have the strength to hold up the dough. A rye dough tends to spread outwards rather than upwards, so that rye flour must be used with discretion. Buckwheat is ordinarily used only for pancakes and blinis because of its very unusual taste.

There are many other flours used in yeast breads which have no gluten at all. These include corn-meal, oats, and soy flour. When you add them to a yeast dough, they do not rise. In effect, they are dead weights. This does not mean that you cannot or should not use them. You can use them, but they should not account for more than one-sixth the total volume of flour. (For example, a typical white bread dough producing two loaves of bread contains six cups of flour. You could successfully substitute one cup of oats for one cup of white flour.)

When measuring flour for yeast doughs, do not sift the flour, simply scoop it up into dry measure cups and level it off with a knife. It does not matter whether the flour is white or whole-grain. Once you become adept at making yeast doughs, you will probably dispense with leveling off each cup of flour. With a quick flick of the wrist, the cup will be sufficiently leveled.

When measuring honey, molasses, and other sticky liquids, lightly but thoroughly oil the measuring cup before adding the honey or molasses. The full amount of liquid will pour out of the cup with ease.

Glutenous Grain Breads

White Bread

Yield: Two 9-by-5-inch loaves

This recipe will produce two large, lightweight breads with a very luxurious taste. If you have been disappointed by the tastelessness and lack of texture in commercial white breads, try this one. The ingredients that make it taste special are the butter and honey. Commercial breads are generally made with shortening and sugar. You will notice that the butter and honey are present in rather small quantities; however, their taste is delightfully apparent in the finished bread. This amplification of taste is one of the marvelous properties of yeast. If you made a non-yeast bread or cake of the same weight as this recipe, with the same amount of butter and honey, the result would be insipid.

The fine texture of this bread owes its moistness to the potatoes, its lightness to the limited amount of flour, and its fine grain to three risings.

1¾ cups milk
4 tablespoons (¼ cup) sweet butter
1 tablespoon salt
1 cup hot mashed potatoes
 (1 medium-sized potato)
¼ cup honey
1 ounce fresh yeast (or 2 packages
 dry yeast, proofed — see p. 8)
¼ cup cool water
6 cups unbleached, all-purpose flour

Heat 1 cup of the milk and pour it over the butter and salt in a large bowl. Add the hot mashed potatoes, blending them in with a large wire whisk or a wooden spoon. When the butter is melted, add the rest of the milk and the honey. Allow the mixture to cool to about room temperature. Meanwhile, dissolve the yeast in the cool water and let it stand for 5 minutes. Then add the yeast to the liquid mixture in the bowl. Beat in 4 cups of the flour, 1 cup at a time. If you are using a whisk, switch to a spoon after 2 or 3 cups, because the whisk will get clogged.

Although the dough may seem terribly soft at this stage, it is nearly time to turn it out of the bowl, because the softer the dough, the more fluffy the finished bread will be. Have the remaining 2 cups of flour ready to use as follows: Sprinkle ½ cup flour around the edge of the dough in the bowl and another ¼ cup flour onto your kneading cloth. Rub the flour into the cloth. Use a wooden spoon to work the flour underneath the

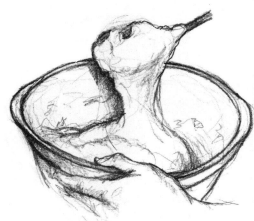

dough, by moving your spoon in downward strokes around the sides of the bowl. Turn the bowl over, and the dough will fall out onto your floured kneading surface. Sprinkle ¼ cup flour over the dough and work the dough into one homogeneous mass by turning it over and over on the floured cloth, lifting it gently with the sides of your hands. (I call this process prekneading.) The dough is very soft and sticky, so be sure not to put your fingers into it, for they will get stuck. In a minute or so, the dough will feel less sticky and you can start to knead heartily.

Use the 1 cup of flour that is left, a little at a time, to flour the cloth each time the dough seems to be getting sticky. Turn the dough around on the floured cloth to lightly powder its surface. To knead, push and stretch the dough from the center outwards, with the heels of your hands; flip the dough in half and quickly flip the whole mass over. Repeat this process for about 5 minutes, flouring the cloth as necessary, then rolling the dough around on the floured cloth.

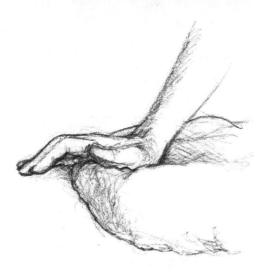

In order to avoid adding too much flour, which will create very heavy bread, it will be helpful to follow these guidelines for when and where to add flour while kneading, using the flour from the sixth cup:

1. Keep your hands well floured.

2. Keep the kneading area well floured. When you add flour to the area, turn your dough around on it. This will lightly flour the surface of your dough and make it unsticky.

3. If the dough has become hopelessly sticky, you may flour the dough directly, but flour only that part of the dough that you are actually going to touch. While you push and stretch the dough in the kneading process, you will constantly be exposing sticky spots. That is why you fold it in half — to get them back inside the dough mass, to hide them. Once you have created sticky spots, do not touch them again. Fold them in. Turn the dough over and start pushing and stretching another surface. In other words, do not put flour on a sticky spot and then immediately fold the dough in half. If you do, you will only have folded unused flour into your dough. Doing this repeatedly creates heavy bread.

Rising of the Dough: First and Second Rises

After kneading for about 5 minutes, the dough will feel springy and pop back at you when you press it with your finger. Place the dough in a well-oiled bowl. Turn the dough in the bowl so that it becomes lightly filmed with oil. Cover the bowl with a damp towel. Place it to rise in a draft-free place, at room temperature, until the dough almost doubles in bulk (approximately 1 hour).

Punch the dough down in the bowl and turn it out onto your floured kneading surface. Knead it for another 5 minutes. Re-oil the bowl if necessary, replace the dough in it, turn the dough to lightly oil its surface, and allow it to rise a second time (approximately 45 minutes to 1 hour, or until almost doubled in bulk).

After the dough has risen for the second time, punch it down, turn it out onto the floured kneading surface, and knead it for a few minutes. With a sharp knife, cut the dough in half for two loaves. This recipe makes two 9-by-5-inch loaves. (You may also use a 2-quart round casserole in place of a loaf pan.) Grease the pans thoroughly, using solid vegetable shortening,

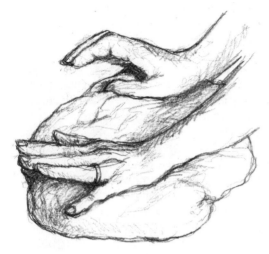

and then sprinkle in some flour. Knock the flour about to make an even coating, and then knock out the excess.

Shaping of the Dough and the Third Rise

To shape the loaves, simply work each piece of dough into a smooth ball and place it in the prepared pan. It does not matter if the dough does not come to the end of the pan; it will all even out in the rising. Cover the pans with a towel and let the breads rise until they are about an inch above the tops of the pans, approximately triple in bulk (rising time about 1 hour). If the dough has not quite tripled in an hour, allow it a bit more time. What is of importance is the size of the bread, not the length of the time that it has been rising.

Glazing and Baking

Brush the tops of the loaves with melted butter, and bake the breads on the bottom rung of a preheated 350-degree oven for 30 to 35 minutes (in oven-glass pans; metal pans will take about 40 minutes). To test for doneness, tap the loaves — they should sound hollow. Also a toothpick inserted into the fattest part of the loaf should come out bone dry.

Immediately upon removing the breads from the oven, turn them out of the pans onto wire racks. Allow the breads to cool thoroughly for 2 to 3 hours before eating or wrapping.

Whole Wheat Bread

Yield: Two 9-by-5-inch loaves

This recipe for whole wheat bread follows the format of the white bread recipe. Within the six-cup flour allowance, feel free to vary the proportion of whole wheat flour to white. My measurements are four cups whole wheat and two cups white, which gives you 66⅔ percent whole wheat bread. The reason I use white flour at all is that it is much easier to knead with than whole wheat. For a very lightweight whole wheat bread, use only one or two cups of whole wheat flour.

1¾ cups milk
4 tablespoons (¼ cup) sweet butter
1 tablespoon salt
1 cup hot mashed potatoes
   (1 medium-sized potato)
¼ cup honey or unsulphured
   molasses
1 ounce fresh yeast (or 2 packages
   dry yeast, proofed — see p. 8)
¼ cup cool water
4 cups stone-ground whole
   wheat flour
2 cups unbleached all-purpose flour

Heat 1 cup of the milk and pour it over the butter and salt in a large bowl. Add the hot mashed potatoes, blending them in with a large wire whisk or a wooden spoon. When the butter is melted, add the rest of the milk and the honey or molasses. Allow the mixture to cool to about room temperature. Meanwhile, dissolve the yeast in the cool water and let it stand for 5 minutes. Then add the yeast to the liquid mixture in the bowl. Beat in the whole wheat flour, 1 cup at a time. If you are using a whisk, switch to a spoon after 2 or 3 cups, because the whisk will get clogged.

Following the instructions for dislodging the dough from the bowl in the White Bread recipe, sprinkle ½ cup of the white flour around the edge of the dough and work the flour underneath the dough with a wooden spoon. Rub ¼ cup flour onto your kneading cloth. Turn the dough out of the bowl onto the cloth and sprinkle it with ¼ cup additional flour. Work the dough into one homogenous mass by turning it over and over on the floured cloth, lifting it gently with the sides of your hands (prekneading). Then knead the dough for about 5 minutes, using the amount necessary from the remaining 1 cup of flour.

Allow the dough 2 rises in an oiled bowl. Each rise will take about an hour. Knead the dough for about 3 to 5 minutes between the rises. After the second rise, knead for a few minutes and cut the dough in half. Form each half into a smooth ball and place each in a greased and floured loaf pan. Allow the dough to rise a third time until doubled in bulk. (Whole wheat flour is heavy and will not triple. If you have used only 1 or 2 cups of whole wheat flour, allow the bread to rise to 2½ times its original bulk.)

Glaze the risen breads with melted butter, if desired, and bake them in a preheated 350-degree oven for 30 to 35 minutes (in oven-glass pans; metal pans will take about 40 minutes). To test for doneness, tap the loaves — they should sound hollow. Also, a toothpick inserted into the fattest part of the loaf should come out bone dry.

Immediately upon removing the breads from the oven, turn them out of the pans onto wire racks. Allow them to cool for 2 to 3 hours before eating or wrapping.

Challah

Yield: Two 9-by-5-inch braids, or two round loaves, or one large braid

Challah is the special egg bread which is always prepared for the Jewish Sabbath and for many holidays. The dough is braided for Sabbath, but for holidays it is often baked as a round spiral, sometimes with raisins added. Challah is usually served with all meals on the Sabbath, and because of the dietary laws which strictly forbid the consumption of dairy products at a meat meal, challah is made with oil and water rather than with butter and milk. Aside from these ingredient changes, challah is very similar to brioche (see the Advanced Techniques Section).

If you bake the challah in pans (either loaf or round), you may keep the dough very soft, and the resulting bread will be extraordinarily light and fluffy. However, challah is traditionally baked as a free-form braid on a baking sheet, where there are no pan sides to support a soft dough. If you want to bake challah in this free-form manner, you must add extra flour to the dough so that the total flour used is six cups. Then the dough will be stiff enough to support itself on a baking sheet. Complete instructions for shaping challah, in both kinds of pans, and on baking sheets, are at the end of the recipe.

1 cup water (if you have boiled a
   potato, use the potato water — it
   contains many nutrients)
¼ cup corn oil (or other tasteless
   salad oil)
1 tablespoon salt
1 cup hot mashed potatoes
   (1 medium-sized potato)
8 egg yolks
½ cup honey
1 ounce fresh yeast (or 2 packages
   dry yeast, proofed — see p. 8)
¼ cup cool water
5-5½ cups unbleached all-purpose
   flour (6 cups for a free-form loaf)

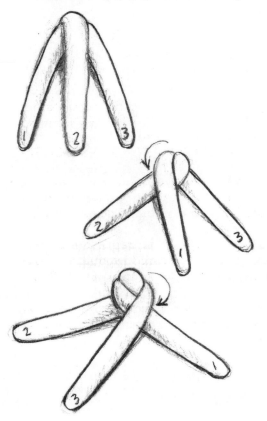

Combine the water, oil, salt, potatoes, egg yolks, and honey in a large bowl. Cool this mixture until it is about room temperature. Dissolve the yeast in the cool water and let it stand for 5 minutes; then combine the yeast mixture with the liquid mixture in the bowl.

Beat in 4 cups of flour (4½ cups for free-form), 1 cup at a time. (You may start with a large wire whisk, but change to a large wooden spoon after 2 or 3 cups, because the whisk will get clogged.)

Following the instructions for dislodging the dough from the bowl in the White Bread recipe, sprinkle ½ cup flour around the edge of the dough and work the flour underneath the dough with a wooden spoon. Rub ¼ cup flour onto your kneading cloth. Turn the dough out of the bowl onto the cloth and sprinkle it with ¼ cup additional flour. Work the dough into one homogeneous mass by turning it over and over on the floured cloth, lifting it gently with the sides of your hands (prekneading). Then knead the dough for about 5 minutes, using the amount necessary from the remaining ½ cup of flour. (For breads baked in pans use as little as you can of this ½ cup flour; however, for the free-form breads, knead in all of it, to make the dough stiffer.)

Allow the dough 2 rises in an oiled bowl. Each rise will take about an hour. Knead the dough for about 3 to 5 minutes between the rises. After the second rise, knead the dough for a few minutes, and the dough will be ready to be shaped by one of the methods that follow.

1. Braids Shaped in Loaf Pans

Cut the dough in half. (Each half will produce one braided loaf.) Cut each half into 3 pieces and lightly flour the cut sides of the dough to avoid excessive sticking. Cover the dough with a cloth, and let it rest for about 15 to 20 minutes to allow the gluten to relax. Relaxed dough is much easier to shape because it does not keep bouncing back at you. During this rest period, grease and flour the loaf pans.

For each braid, form 3 of the pieces of dough into ropes about 11 or 12 inches long. Arrange them on the kneading cloth facing you. Place the tops of the 2 outside ropes underneath the middle one and pull the top of the middle rope over them and underneath to seal the 3 ropes together. Now

you are ready to braid. Simply pull an outside rope over the center rope, and then the opposite outside rope over the center rope. (Notice that each rope becomes the next center rope as it is pulled over.) Be sure that you are making the braid tight; do not leave large air spaces between the strands. When you come to the end, seal the bottom just as you did the top — pull the center rope over and underneath the others. Now you have a braid that is probably over a foot long, and your loaf pan is only 9 inches long. To make it fit, fold both ends of the braid underneath to meet in the center, and you will have a compact loaf about 6 inches long. Place it in the loaf pan and do not worry that the braid does not fill the pan either lengthwise or widthwise. It will eventually fill the pan as it rises. Cover the dough with a cloth to allow the dough to triple in bulk, which will take 1 to 1½ hours. Then proceed with glazing and baking (see p. 33).

2. *Round Challahs Baked in 2-Quart Casseroles*

(If you wish to add raisins to your round challah, knead ¾ cup raisins into the dough for each loaf [or 1½ cups raisins for both loaves] after the second rise.)

Divide the dough in half (each half will produce one round loaf), and lightly flour the cut surfaces to avoid excessive sticking. Cover the dough with a cloth, and let it rest for 15 to 20 minutes to relax the gluten. During this rest period, grease and flour the casseroles.

For each round loaf, form each half of the dough into a long rope, about 20 to 25 inches long. You may either form the loaf by making it into a knot or by snaking it around into a spiral, as follows:

a. To form a knot, hold one end of the rope in each hand and form a circle. Pull one end of the rope over and underneath the other, and then up through the center to make a head. Place it in the casserole.

b. To spiral the dough around, simply place one end of the dough on the cloth and form a circle about 6 inches in

diameter that does not quite meet, and continue to make increasingly smaller circles within the original, until the dough is used up. (You will be able to spiral around about 3 times, and the last end will be a little lump on the top.) Place the dough in the casserole.

Cover the dough with a cloth and allow the dough to triple in bulk, which will take 1 to 1½ hours. Then proceed with glazing and baking (see p. 33).

3. A Very Large Three-Tiered Free-Form Braid Made from All the Dough

Make the dough with all 6 cups of flour so that the bread will hold its shape. Divide the dough in half. Cut one piece into 3 parts, flour the cut surfaces, and set aside, covered with a cloth. This section will constitute the base or the first braided tier.

Divide the remaining dough into 2 uneven parts, one part about twice as big as the other. The larger part will become the second braided tier. Divide it in 3, flour the cut surfaces, and set aside. Divide the small part in 3 (this will be the third tier), flour the cut surfaces, and set aside. Allow the dough to relax for 15 to 20 minutes. During this rest period prepare the baking sheet as follows. (An 11-by-15-inch jelly-roll pan is a good size.) Grease it thoroughly with solid vegetable shortening and sprinkle it liberally with cornmeal or farina, knocking it about to coat the pan evenly. Then knock out the excess. The cornmeal or farina offers a little more protection than flour does from bottom-burning, and because this large bread takes longer to bake than challahs in loaf pans, you will be sure not to have an overdone bottom.

Form the 3 largest pieces of dough, which will constitute the base, into ropes and braid them, following the instructions for the braided loaf — but do not fold the ends underneath the finished braid. Simply lay the braid flat on the baking sheet.

Now form the second tier pieces of dough into ropes, the same length as for the bigger braid, because this braid should be the same length, although it will be thinner. Braid these ropes. Take a pair of scissors and cut a shallow trough down the center of the large braid on the baking sheet. Place the second braid in this trough and stretch the ends a bit so that you can seal them under the first braid.

Take the smallest pieces of dough, form them into long, thin ropes. (This braid will be very thin and should be a bit longer

than the other 2 so that its ends can be stretched to seal them under the base braid.) Braid the ropes. Cut a shallow trough, with the scissors, down the center of the second-tier braid and place this third braid in the trough. Stretch the ends so that you can seal them underneath the bread.

Cover the bread with a cloth and allow it to triple in bulk (about 1½ hours). Then proceed with the glazing and baking, below.

Glazing and Baking

When the dough is fully risen, preheat the oven to 325 degrees and set the oven rung in the lowest position. Glaze the loaves with 1 egg beaten with 2 tablespoons of water. Challahs in loaf pans or casseroles will take 30 to 35 minutes to bake in glass pans and about 40 minutes in metal.

For the very large three-tiered braid, place it in the oven and bake it for 10 minutes. Then lightly lay a piece of aluminum foil over the bread and continue to bake it for 35 to 45 minutes more. (Total baking time will be 45 to 55 minutes.) If, toward the end of the baking, the bread is not browning, remove the foil.

The breads are done when a toothpick inserted into the fattest part of the loaf comes out bone dry. They will also sound hollow when tapped. (Beware: the breads may sound hollow on top before the insides are cooked — the test is really that the bottom sounds hollow, but by then your breads have already been unmolded. Rely more heavily on the toothpick test, especially with the large braid.)

As soon as the breads are done, unmold them and allow them to cool on wire racks. To unmold the large bread from the baking sheet, use 2 pancake flippers to transfer it to the rack. The loaves need at least 2 hours to cool before eating or wrapping, and the large bread needs a minimum of 3 hours.

Limpa

Limpa is a soft, whole-grain rye bread of Swedish origin that is flavored with grated orange rind. Because the bread is slightly sweet, it is best served for breakfast or for tea, with sweet butter. If you are a connoisseur of freshly ground peanut butter, this is the bread to spread it on.

1¾ cups milk
4 tablespoons sweet butter
1 tablespoon salt
1 cup hot mashed potatoes
⅓-½ cup unsulphured molasses, depending on if you want the bread slightly sweet or a bit sweeter, like a coffee cake
Grated rind of 2 large navel oranges
1 ounce fresh yeast (or 2 packages dry yeast, proofed — see p. 8)
¼ cup cool water
2 cups whole rye flour
2 cups whole wheat flour
2 cups unbleached all-purpose white flour

Heat 1 cup of the milk and pour it over the butter and salt in a large bowl. Add the hot mashed potatoes, blending them in with a large wire whisk or a wooden spoon. When the butter is melted, add the rest of the milk, the molasses, and the orange rind. Allow the mixture to cool to about room temperature. Meanwhile, dissolve the yeast in the cool water and let it stand for 5 minutes. Then add the yeast to the liquid mixture in the bowl. Beat in the rye flour, then the whole wheat flour, using a wooden spoon.

Following the instructions for dislodging the dough from the bowl in the White Bread recipe, sprinkle ½ cup white flour around the edge of the dough and work the flour underneath the dough with a wooden spoon. Rub ¼ cup flour onto your kneading cloth. Turn the dough out of the bowl onto the cloth and sprinkle it with ¼ cup additional flour. Work the dough into one homogeneous mass by turning it over and over on the floured cloth, lifting it gently with the sides of your hands (prekneading). Then knead the dough for about 5 minutes, using the amount necessary of the remaining 1 cup of flour.

Allow the dough 2 rises in an oiled bowl. Each rise will take about 1 to 1¼ hours. Knead the dough for about 3 to 5 minutes between the rises. After the second rise, knead for a few minutes and cut the dough in half. Form each half into a smooth ball and place each into a greased and floured loaf pan. Allow the dough to rise a third time until doubled in bulk. (Whole-grain flours are heavy and will not triple.)

Glaze the risen breads with melted butter, if desired, and bake them in a preheated 350-degree oven for 30 to 35 minutes (in oven glass pans; metal will take about 40 minutes). To test for doneness, tap the loaves — they should sound hollow.

Immediately upon removing the breads from the oven, turn them out of the pans onto wire racks. Allow them to cool for 2 to 3 hours before eating or wrapping.

Water Bread

Almost all bread-eating cultures make use of a simple dough made of flour, water, yeast, and salt. The most familiar of these breads to us are French- or Italian-type loaves. Other breads that are made of this dough include pizza and bagels.

These breads may have had their beginnings in frugality (note that there is no butter, eggs, milk, sugar, honey, or other expensive ingredient in the dough), but that is not the major reason for our interest in them today. These breads are absolutely delicious. Properly made, they are crusty on the outside, and wonderfully chewy on the inside. Because the dough is not sweetened, these breads can be served with any kind of food.

There are a few problems involved with baking French or Italian breads in your home oven. A European baker's oven is made out of stone on which the bread is directly baked. Home ovens are made of enameled steel, and you must use baking sheets, unless you line your oven with tiles. A European baker's oven is also equipped with a steam contraption that releases gushes of hot steam into the oven at intervals during the baking; this is responsible for creating the crunchy crust on these loaves. You can, however, place a pan of boiling water on the oven floor and squirt the bread with water from an atomizer or a clean spray bottle. This helps quite a bit. Reheating homemade French or Italian breads before serving makes the crusts really crunchy. (Garlic bread made from these loaves will be superb.)

If you would really like to try to simulate a French baker's oven, you must read the wonderful chapter on French bread in Julia Child's Mastering the Art of French Cooking, Volume II. *If you have ever been to France, you undoubtedly remember the joy of tearing off a piece of baguette, fresh from the bakery. There is no taste in the world quite like it. By following Julia Child's procedure, you can come closer to producing the real thing than by any other method, using an American home oven and American flour.*

The French or Italian bread recipe that appears in this chapter will produce good, crusty loaves of the kind that we are accustomed to in America. It is a simpler recipe than the one in Mastering, *and the results are very satisfactory, although not authentic. As for the bagel and pizza recipes in this section, I am sure you will be pleased. The pizza comes out of the oven crusty, with its top bubbling, and the bagels are properly chewy. Their texture is due to the initial boiling of the dough before baking.*

For the French or Italian bread, the dough requires three rises, so that the texture of the crumb may develop. The pizza and bagels require only two rises and can really be produced quite fast — for yeast doughs. You will note that there are no potatoes in this recipe. Potatoes would produce too tender a dough; the object here is to make a chewy texture.

This is a large recipe. If you do not want such a large quantity of bread, pizza, or bagels in one day, freeze half the dough after the first rise, or just make half the recipe.

WATER DOUGH

1 ounce fresh yeast (or 2 packages dry yeast, proofed; see p. 8)
2½ cups cool water
2½ teaspoons salt
6 cups unbleached, all-purpose white flour

Dissolve the yeast in the cool water in a large mixing bowl. Let it stand for 5 minutes. Then stir in the salt. Add 5 cups of the flour, 1 cup at a time, beating after each addition.

Following the instructions for dislodging the dough from the bowl in the White Bread recipe, sprinkle ¼ cup flour around the edge of the dough and work the flour underneath the dough with a wooden spoon. Rub ¼ cup flour onto your kneading cloth. Turn the dough out of the bowl onto the cloth and sprinkle it with ¼ cup additional flour. Work the dough into one homogeneous mass by turning it over and over on the floured cloth, lifting it gently with the sides of your hands (prekneading). Knead the dough thoroughly for 10 minutes, using the remaining ¼ cup of flour as necessary. This dough is not soft, like the white bread dough; it is rather firm, but it still may become sticky. If you feel that the dough is too sticky to knead thoroughly for 10 minutes, you can use an additional ¼ cup flour — sparingly. Rub some of the extra flour onto the kneading cloth, and then roll the dough around on the floured surface. This will make better use of the flour than if you add it to the dough directly. This process may be repeated as necessary with the remainder of the extra flour.

Set the dough to rise at room temperature in a lightly floured bowl. (Do not oil the bowl — oil will ruin the crust.) Cover the bowl with a slightly dampened towel. Allow the dough to rise until doubled in bulk, 45 minutes to 1 hour.

For bagels and pizza you may proceed with the recipe after the first rise; see directions below. For French or Italian loaves, punch the dough down, turn it onto the kneading cloth, and knead it again for 5 minutes. Replace the dough in the floured bowl (reflouring if necessary) and allow it to rise again until doubled in bulk (45 minutes to 1 hour). Then proceed with the directions below.

FRENCH OR ITALIAN LOAVES

Yield: Four 3-by-5-inch loaves

After the second rise; again punch the dough down, turn it out onto the kneading cloth, and knead it for 5 minutes. Cut the dough into 4 equal pieces. Allow the dough to rest for about 15 minutes to relax the gluten.

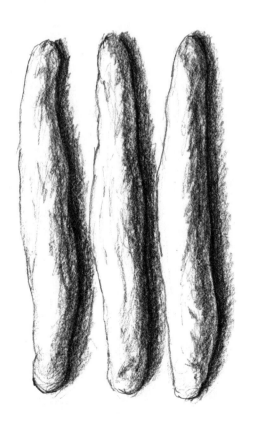

You will need 2 baking sheets that measure about 11 by 17 inches. Two loaves will bake on each sheet. If your oven is large and you can accommodate both sheets side by side on the same shelf of the oven, then all 4 loaves can be baked at the same time. However, if only 1 sheet at a time fits on the shelf, you should refrigerate 2 pieces of the dough for about 40 minutes. Then take them out and set them up to rise. The first 2 loaves will be out of the oven when the next 2 are ready to go in. During the resting period, prepare the rising cloths necessary for the final rise.

For each loaf you will need 2 cloths that are about 4 inches longer than the shaped loaves. Linen dish towels, cut-up sheets or clean diapers are fine. One cloth will be dampened; the other cloth will be dry and floured. You will also need some heavy books or kitchen utensils to hold the ends of your cloths on the table, as you suspend the rising bread.

Shaping and the Third Rise

To shape each loaf, lengthen a piece of dough by rolling it back and forth against the kneading cloth with the palms of your hands. Be sure that you do not make it longer than 15 inches, or it will not fit on the baking sheet. The ends should taper somewhat. Place a dry cloth on top of a damp one. Rub some flour into the dry cloth and place your loaf in the center of the 2 cloths. Pick up the ends of the cloths so that the dough hangs in the middle, and suspend the whole assembly from a table top, using the heavy books or other weights to hold it in place. This method of rising will allow your loaves to rise upward without spreading out, and creates a perfectly shaped bread. Allow the dough to rise until it is tripled in volume, about 1 to 1½ hours.

Preparations for Baking and Placing Risen Loaves on Baking Sheets

While the dough is rising, prepare the baking sheet by greasing it with solid vegetable shortening and sprinkling it heavily with cornmeal or farina. Fill a clean atomizer or spray bottle with cold water. Have several quarts of boiling water ready to fill a large pan that will sit on the oven floor. Place the oven rack in the middle level of the oven. When the dough is about risen, preheat the oven to 425 degrees and place the large pan on the oven floor. Pour in the boiling water to a depth of

about 1 to 1½ inches. This will start to steam up the oven before the breads are placed inside. (If you notice during the baking that the water is evaporating, replace it with additional boiling water. Do not let the pan burn.)

To place the risen loaf on the baking sheet, carefully remove the weights from the cloths while holding on to them firmly. Holding the cloths tautly, directly over the baking sheet, roll the loaf off the cloths and onto the sheet. (This is really very easy. However, the first time you try it perhaps you could borrow another set of hands. If an assistant removes the weights as you hold the cloths, and then holds the baking sheet steady as you roll on the loaf, you might feel more secure.) Repeat the process to place the second loaf on the same baking sheet.

Slash the risen loaves diagonally 3 or 4 times with a razor blade or a very, very sharp knife. Glaze the loaves gently with cold water, using a pastry brush.

Baking the Bread

Place the loaves on the middle level of the hot oven and close the oven door. After 5 minutes, open the oven and quickly squirt the breads with water from the atomizer or spray bottle. Close the door. Repeat the squirting every 5 minutes for 20 minutes (a total of 4 squirtings) and be sure not to let the pan of water boil away. Replace it with more boiling water as necessary. The bread will take 30 to 35 minutes to bake. The crust should be nicely browned, and the bread should sound hollow when tapped.

Immediately upon removing the breads from the oven, remove them from the baking sheet and allow them to cool on wire racks for 2 or 3 hours before eating. (This bread becomes stale quickly and should be eaten the day it is made. If it is to be eaten the same day, it should not be wrapped, because the crust will become soggy.)

PIZZA

Yield: Two large rectangular pizzas about 11 by 17-inches

Pizza dough is baked in an unrisen state. It is allowed to rise once before being deflated and shaped, which develops the characteristic flavor of the dough.

If it fits your time schedule better, you certainly can allow the dough to rise again before turning it into pizza.

HAVE READY FOR EACH PIZZA:

The risen dough, still in its rising bowl

About 1-1½ cups of well-flavored marinara sauce, highly seasoned with oregano and basil

¾ pound mozzarella cheese, grated

OPTIONAL INGREDIENTS:

Freshly grated Parmesan cheese
Sautéed mushrooms
Sautéed onions
Roasted or sautéed peppers
Pepperoni, sliced thin

For each pizza, grease an 11-by-17-inch (or slightly larger) baking sheet with solid vegetable shortening. There is no need to flour the pan. Preheat the oven to 425 degrees. Place the oven rack in the lowest position.

Without punching the dough, simply knock it out of the bowl onto the kneading cloth. Do not knead the dough. Kneading would activate the gluten and make the dough hard to stretch out into a large area. If you have dough for 2 pizzas, take a long serrated knife and swiftly cut the still risen dough in half. If you are not baking both pizzas at the same time, quickly deflate half the dough with 2 or 3 fast punches and refrigerate it until used — up to 1½ hours. (Do not in any way knead or work this dough unless you plan to freeze it. In that case, you should knead the dough and then freeze it.)

Use a rolling pin to start rolling the still risen dough into a rectangle. The action of rolling will deflate the dough. Then, with your hands, stretch and pull the dough to slightly larger dimensions than the size of your baking sheet. Lift up the dough and fit it on the sheet. Crimp the edges all around the pan to form a border that will enclose the ingredients. If there are edges that are too thick or long, cut them off with a pair of scissors or a knife. You can use these extra pieces of dough to patch any spot that might have become too thin.

Spread the sauce on the pizza. If your sauce is very thick, you will probably need the entire 1½ cups; if it is thin, 1 cup will suffice. Sprinkle the sauce with Parmesan cheese, if desired. Then evenly spread the mozzarella cheese over the sauce. If you are using mushrooms, onions, peppers, and/or pepperoni, place them over the mozzarella.

Place the pizza in the oven and bake it for about 20 minutes, or until the crust is brown and the topping bubbles. Allow the pizza to cool for about 5 minutes before serving, so that you do not burn your guests.

BAGELS

If you cannot fit all 16 to 18 bagels on the top shelf of the oven at the same time, do not panic. Once boiled, the yeast is killed and there is no more rising action. One set of boiled bagels can safely wait on a prepared baking sheet until the other set comes out of the oven.

In an oven that I once had, I simply could not get the bagels to brown, no matter how long I baked them. To solve the problem, I glazed the boiled bagels with a mixture of one egg yolk mixed with one tablespoon water before baking.

After the dough has risen once, punch it down and turn it out onto the kneading cloth. Knead the dough for about 5 minutes and then divide it into 16 to 18 pieces. Let the dough rest for about 15 minutes to relax the gluten. Meanwhile, prepare a floured board upon which the bagels will rise. Letting them rise on a board, rather than on the taped-down kneading cloth, makes it easier to transport them to the stove for boiling.

Roll each piece of dough back and forth against the kneading cloth into a thin rope about 11 or 12 inches long. Form each rope into a well-sealed ring that is about 4 to 5 inches in diameter. Wind the ends of the rope around the ring several times to form a seal. Place the rings on the floured board and cover them with a dry towel. Allow them to rise until they are about 2½ times their original bulk.

While they are rising, fill 1 or 2 wide pots with water to a depth of 3 inches or more and bring to a boil. Grease 2 or 3 cookie sheets with solid vegetable shortening and sprinkle them with cornmeal or farina. Prepare some wire racks on platters, pans, or plates, to drain the bagels after boiling. When the dough is risen, preheat the oven to 425 degrees and place the oven rack in the highest position.

When the dough is risen, plunge in as many rings as can fit comfortably. Boil them for 1 to 2 minutes on each side. Remove them from the water with pancake flippers and allow them to drain on the wire racks. Boil the remaining rings. Place the bagels (once boiled, they can be called bagels) on the prepared baking sheets and bake them for about 30 to 35 minutes, until nicely browned. Cool the bagels for about 15 minutes on wire racks before serving.

Rolls

Any of the basic bread recipes can be made into rolls. Rolls can be baked either in greased and floured muffin pans or on baking sheets. A half of any one of the bread recipes will produce about 18 to 24 rolls. Here are some guidelines to follow that will make roll baking very easy:

1. If you want to bake rolls in a hurry, you may omit the potatoes. These rolls should be eaten the day they are baked.

2. If you are making dough specifically for rolls, you need only allow it 2 risings (one in the bowl and one in its shape on the baking pan). Of course, you can allow the usual 3 risings. Since the volume of a roll is small, an uneven texture in the crumb is not as noticeable as in a slice from a large loaf.

3. Rolls should be baked in the upper third of your oven, at about 375 degrees. Small-sized doughs are always baked high in the oven to prevent bottom-burning, and to allow the tops to brown during the very short baking period. Rolls take from 10 to 20 minutes to bake. They are done when they are nicely browned. Cool rolls on a wire rack.

4. Rolls made with white flour may be eaten after a cooling period of only 10 to 15 minutes. Because rolls are small, the heavy moisture content evaporates much faster than from large breads. Rolls made with whole grains should be allowed to cool for at least 30 to 45 minutes before eating, because whole-grain flours hold moisture much longer than white flour. (See page 14, "Cooling Yeast Breads and Cakes.")

5. For crusty rolls, bake them on a greased and cornmealed baking sheet. Use a dough that has no fat in it, such as the Water Bread, Pumpernickel I, or Rye Bread. Place a pan of boiling water on the oven floor to create steam throughout the baking. Glaze the risen rolls with cold water, or with an egg white that has been beaten with 2 tablespoons of water. The best shape for a crusty roll is a simple round ball. Be sure to shape the pumpernickel or rye rolls very high, since they tend to flatten out a bit. Slash the risen rolls once or twice with a sharp knife or razor blade before glazing.

Shaping Soft Rolls

There are many ways to shape rolls. Here are a few suggestions:
CLOVERLEAF ROLLS: For each roll, form 3 little balls and place them in a greased and floured muffin cup.

KNOTS: For each roll, form the dough into a rope about 9 inches long. Tie it into a knot and tuck the ends underneath.

SANDWICH BUNS OR HAMBURGER ROLLS: Allow the kneaded dough to rest for about 15 minutes to relax the gluten. Roll the dough out on the floured pastry cloth to a thickness of about ⅓ inch and cut out rounds with a 3½- to 4-inch cutter.

SPIRALS: Allow the kneaded dough to rest for about 15 minutes to relax the gluten. Roll the dough out thin on the floured pastry cloth. Brush the dough heavily with cooled melted butter. If desired, sprinkle it with cinnamon-sugar. Roll the dough like a jelly roll and cut off 1-inch slices. Place the spirals on a greased and floured baking sheet or in muffin cups.

PULL-APART ROLLS: See the directions in the following recipe for rolls that are baked in a round pan touching one another.

Extra-Rich, Quick, Soft Dinner Rolls
Yield: 18 to 30 rolls

These are the buttery, soft, warm rolls of your childhood dreams. They can be ready to eat about 2½ hours after you start preparing them. That is mighty fast for a yeast dough! A simple dinner will become a party with rolls hot from the oven. Serve them in a linen-lined basket.

1½ cups milk
6 tablespoons butter
2 teaspoons salt
¼ cup honey
1 ounce fresh yeast (or 2 packages dry yeast, proofed; see p. 8)
¼ cup cool water
4½ cups unbleached, all-purpose white flour

Heat ½ cup of the milk and the butter in a pan until the butter is melted. Pour it into a large mixing bowl. Add the salt, the rest of the milk, and the honey. The mixture should be about room temperature. If it is hotter, allow it to cool.

Dissolve the yeast in the cool water in a cup. Allow it to stand for 5 minutes. Then add it to the liquid mixture in the bowl. Stir in 3½ cups of the flour.

Following the instructions for dislodging the dough from the bowl in the White Bread recipe, sprinkle ¼ cup flour around the edge of the dough and work the flour underneath it with a wooden spoon. Rub ¼ cup flour onto your kneading cloth. Turn the dough out of the bowl onto the cloth and sprinkle it with ¼ cup additional flour. Work the dough into one homogeneous mass by turning it over and over on the floured cloth, lifting it gently with the sides of your hands (prekneading). Then knead the dough for about 3 minutes, using the amount necessary of the remaining ¼ cup of flour. Keep the dough as soft as possible for fluffy rolls.

Shaping Pull-Apart Rolls in a Round Pan

Grease and flour 2 9- or 10-inch pie pans or 2 1½- to 2-quart round casseroles. Divide the dough in half. Each half of the dough will fill 1 pan or casserole. Cut each half of the dough into 10 to 15 pieces. Shape each little piece into a ball by rolling it around on the pastry cloth or in the palms of your hands.

For extra-buttery rolls, dip each ball into cooled, melted butter. Place the balls in the pans, and allow the dough to rise until it is triple its original volume. As the rolls rise, they will grow together and become attached.

Preheat the oven to 350 degrees. Place the oven rack in the middle of the oven. If you have not dipped each roll in butter previously, brush the tops of the risen dough with cooled, melted butter before baking.

Bake the rolls until they are lightly browned — about 20 to 25 minutes. A toothpick inserted into a middle roll will come out dry.

Upon taking the rolls from the oven, immediately remove them from their pans. To do so, place a wire rack over the pan and invert the pan onto the rack. Remove the pan. Place another rack over the rolls and invert again to turn the rolls right side up. Let the rolls cool about 20 minutes on the racks before serving. Allow your guests to pull off their own rolls.

Non-Glutenous Grain Breads

The breads in the following section (pumpernickels, rye breads, and Cinnamon-Raisin-Oatmeal-Whole Wheat Bread) all contain some amount of grain that will not react with yeast, that will not rise. None of these dead-weight grains constitutes more than one-sixth the total volume of flour in the bread (see page 22). Please note that if you are adding wheat germ or bran to a yeast recipe, they must also be considered dead weights, even though they are parts of wheat. Bran and wheat germ are the non-glutenous parts of the whole wheat grain.

These breads have a special, pleasantly heavy texture, and will only double in volume. In fact, you must be careful not to allow these doughs to stand around too long after they have doubled before baking them, because they tend to become pitted. In other words, they actually start to fall in. If you see any signs of pitting, it is time to bake the bread. (Please do not be so afraid of the dough falling in that you do not let it double; it must completely double in order for the bread to be good.)

Pumpernickels and Ryes

Technically, a pumpernickel is a dark rye bread. But, what makes it darker than ordinary rye bread? This is indeed a loaded question. In principle, it should be a greater proportion of rye flour that makes a pumpernickel darker. (Whole rye flour becomes quite dark in dough.) However, there is a problem with rye flour as we discussed on page 22: Rye flour tends to rise outward rather than upward, which would make very flat, free-form pumpernickels. If you are ever lucky enough to go to an authentic Russian bakery, you will see gigantic wheels of rather flat dark pumpernickel. Unfortunately, this honest bread is not what we Americans are accustomed to. We think of pumpernickel as a very dark, highly risen bread but because of the properties of rye flour, this is impossible. How can the bread be dark and high at the same time? The answer is that it is made dark artificially with coloring agents, such as caramel coloring, bitter chocolate, or coffee powder. The proportion of rye flour in the bread is minute or, in fact, nonexistent. Our commercial pumpernickels, essentially, are colored white breads.

Recipes follow for two basic kinds of pumpernickels — both of them "honest." The first one is baked free-form, and to keep it from becoming flat on the baking sheet, whole wheat flour is used along with the rye. Thus the bread is still high in whole-grain content and does not need coloring agents to make it dark. (It will not be black like a commercial bread, but a nice nutty brown, with all the grains obvious in the crumb of the bread.)

The second kind of pumpernickel is similar to a German Westphalian bread. Because it is almost entirely made of rye flour, it must be baked in loaf pans, and it will be very dark. It should be served in very thin slices and makes a delectable base for hors-d'oeuvre spreads.

All the following recipes for pumpernickels and ryes will take about six hours to complete as written, and they will be lovely breads. However, all these breads are even more robust if done by the Slowing-Up method (see pages 15-18). Using half the yeast and keeping the dough in the refrigerator for three days allows the flavor of the various grains to develop slowly into a very full, hearty taste. When you have mastered the basic techniques, you might enjoy trying this method, especially with the pumpernickels and ryes.

PUMPERNICKEL I

Yield: One large 3½-pound bread or two 1¾-pound breads

1½ cups hot potato water (the water used for boiling the potato)
⅜ cup cornmeal
1 tablespoon salt
1 cup hot mashed potatoes (1 medium-sized potato)
⅓ cup molasses
½ cup 100 percent bran cereal (or unprocessed miller's bran)
1 ounce fresh yeast (or 2 packages dry yeast, proofed; see p. 8)
¼ cup cool water
1½ cups whole rye flour
2 cups whole wheat flour
2½ cups unbleached all-purpose white flour

Pour the potato water gradually over the cornmeal and salt in a large bowl, blending with a large wire whisk to avoid lumps. Blend in the potatoes and the molasses and cool this mixture to room temperature. (It will take some time to cool; you can put it on ice or near a window to speed the process.) Stir in the bran.

When the mixture is ready, dissolve the yeast in the cool water. Let it stand for 5 minutes and then add it to the mixture in the bowl. Stir in the rye flour. Now change from stirring with the whisk to stirring with a large wooden spoon, because the whisk will get clogged. Then stir in the whole wheat flour. Stir in 1½ cups of the white flour. The dough will be extremely stiff at this point. You may want to work the white flour in with your hands, rather than with a spoon, but whichever way, be sure to work it in. This dough is rather weak in gluten, and it is this white flour that will give it body enough to stand up on the baking sheet.

Scrape the dough out of the bowl onto the kneading cloth, and knead with the remaining 1 cup of white flour. Knead in as much of this flour as you can now, and use the rest in the next 2 kneadings. (You will notice that these instructions are contrary to the instructions in the previous recipes and to the introduction, where I caution you about kneading too much flour into the dough. Pumpernickels and ryes are doughs of totally different textures from most other breads, and they require the incorporation of more flour in the mixing and kneading processes so that they will not flatten out.)

Knead the dough for about 10 minutes, to really work up whatever gluten is in the dough.

Rises One and Two

Allow this dough 2 rises in a lightly floured bowl. (Do not oil the bowl, because oil will prevent a crisp crust from forming on the bread when it is baked.) Cover the bowl with a damp cloth. Each rise will take about an hour. Knead the dough for about 5 minutes between the rises.

After the second rise, prepare the baking sheet as follows: For 1 large bread, grease an 11-by-15-inch jelly-roll pan with vegetable shortening. For 2 smaller breads you will need a pan 11 by 17 inches or longer. Sprinkle the pan liberally with cornmeal, knock it about to coat the pan evenly, and then knock out the excess.

Forming the Loaves and the Third Rise

To form the loaf (or loaves), knead the dough heartily for about 5 minutes. Then work the dough into a high, smooth cylinder (5 to 5½ inches high for one large loaf; 4 inches high for the smaller loaves). Roll the cylinder back and forth on the cloth for 2 or 3 minutes, to improve its surface tension. (This helps to keep the dough from flattening out too much.) Place the tall cylinder on the baking sheet. Cover it with a lightly dampened cloth, and allow it to double in bulk.

The bread will double mainly outwards, causing it to flatten somewhat. This is the reason the dough is made into an exaggeratedly tall cylinder; it will end up as a normally high, round loaf.

When the dough is doubled, preheat the oven to 400 degrees and adjust the oven rack to the lowest position.

Glazing, Baking, and Cooling

Glaze the bread with an egg white beaten with 2 tablespoons of water. Bake the large bread 50 to 60 minutes and the smaller ones 35 to 40 minutes. A toothpick inserted into the fattest part of the loaf will come out bone dry.

When the breads are done, remove them immediately from the pans and onto wire racks to cool. The small breads must cool for at least 3 hours before being eaten, and the large loaf must cool for at least 4 hours. Wrapping any bread that has a crisp crust will soften the crust, unfortunately. Therefore, serve the bread the day it is baked. As long as it is not cut open, it can remain unwrapped for 12 hours.

VARIATIONS

CARAWAY PUMPERNICKEL: Add 1 tablespoon whole caraway seeds to the liquid ingredients in the bowl.

RAISIN PUMPERNICKEL: After the second rise, knead 1½ cups raisins into the dough before shaping.

PUMPERNICKEL II

1½ cups hot potato water
⅜ cup cornmeal
1 tablespoon salt
1 cup hot mashed potatoes
   (1 medium-sized potato)
⅓ cup molasses
½ cup 100 percent bran cereal (or
   unprocessed miller's bran)
1 ounce fresh yeast (or 2 packages
   dry yeast, proofed; see p. 8)
¼ cup cool water
4½ cups whole rye flour
1-1½ cups unbleached all-purpose
   white flour

Yield: Two Westphalian-type loaves in 9-by-5-inch loaf pans

Prepare the first 8 ingredients as instructed in Pumpernickel I by gradually combining the potato water with the cornmeal and salt. Blend in the potatoes and the molasses. Cool the mixture to room temperature. Add the bran. Dissolve the yeast in the cool water, let it stand for 5 minutes, and add it to the liquid mixture.

Stir in the rye flour. The mixture will be very stiff. Flour the kneading cloth with some of the white flour, scrape the dough out onto the cloth, and knead the dough for about 10 minutes, using the amount necessary of the white flour. (Although the dough is stiff, it will still be very sticky.)

Allow the dough 2 rises in a lightly floured bowl covered with a damp cloth. Each rise will take about 1 hour. Knead the dough for about 5 minutes between the rises. After the second rise, grease and flour 2 9-by-5-inch loaf pans. Knead the dough for another 5 minutes and cut it in half. Form each half into a smooth elongated oval and place each in its pan. Cover the pans with a damp cloth and allow the dough to rise until

doubled. (The risen dough should be about even with the tops of the pans.) Then preheat the oven to 350 degrees.

You may glaze the dough with an egg white beaten with 2 tablespoons of water, if you want shiny tops. Bake the breads for 40 to 50 minutes, or until a toothpick inserted in the center of the loaf comes out bone dry.

When the breads are done, immediately remove them from the pans and onto wire racks and cool them for about 3 hours before eating or wrapping.

Rye Bread

Yield: One large 3½-pound bread or two 1¾-pound breads

The characteristic flavor of rye bread is caraway. Even when you buy a seedless rye bread, there are finely ground caraway seeds in the dough. Rye flour, on its own, does not produce the flavor that we have come to associate with rye bread. This rye bread recipe follows exactly the same method as Pumpernickel I. There are simply a few variations in the ingredients.

1½ cups hot potato water
½ cup cornmeal
1 tablespoon salt
1 cup hot mashed potatoes
   (1 medium-sized potato)
¼ cup honey
1 tablespoon whole caraway seeds,
   or ½ tablespoon whole and
   ½ tablespoon ground caraway seeds
1 ounce fresh yeast (or 2 packages
   dry yeast, proofed; see p. 8)
¼ cup cool water
1½ cups whole rye flour
4½-5 cups unbleached all-purpose
   white flour

Following the instructions in Pumpernickel I, gradually combine the potato water with the cornmeal and the salt. Blend in the potatoes, honey, and caraway. Cool the mixture to room temperature. Dissolve the yeast in the cool water, let it stand for 5 minutes, and add it to the liquid mixture.

Stir in the rye flour. Stir in 3½ cups of the white flour. (The dough will be very stiff.) Flour the kneading cloth with some of the white flour, and then scrape the dough out onto the cloth. Knead the dough for about 10 minutes, incorporating as much as you can of the remaining 1½ cups of flour. (Save what is left and use it in the next 2 kneadings.)

Follow the instructions for rising, forming the loaves, glazing, baking, and cooling as for Pumpernickel I. Free-form rye breads and pumpernickels are treated in exactly the same way.

VARIATIONS

ONION RYE: Sauté 2 finely minced medium-size onions in as little oil as possible without burning. (A non-stick pan is ideal.) The onions should turn a light golden brown. Cool the onions. Knead them into the dough after the second rise, before shaping.

RAISIN RYE: After the second rise, knead 1½ cups raisins into the dough before shaping.

Cinnamon-Raisin-Oatmeal-Whole Wheat Bread

Yield: Two 9-by-5-inch loaves

This bread was affectionately nicknamed "CROWW Bread" by a grandson of one of my students. What makes it special is that the cinnamon is mixed right in with the dough ingredients. Most cinnamon breads have the cinnamon sprinkled onto the finished rolled-out dough, and then the bread is rolled up like a jelly roll. This is fine, but you may not be lucky enough to get the cinnamon in every bite! With CROWW Bread, every bite gives you the full, abundant flavor of all the ingredients.

Notice that I have omitted potatoes in this recipe, because the oats tend to give the bread moistness. Potatoes in this recipe would make the bread gummy. Note also the use of buttermilk rather than sweet milk. Sweet milk could certainly be used, but buttermilk gives the bread a good tang. Feel free to substitute chopped nuts, dates, or dried figs for the raisins. A combination of dried fruits and nuts is another good idea.

1 cup boiling water
1 tablespoon salt
1 cup rolled oats (either quick-cooking or old-fashioned)
4 tablespoons (½ cup) sweet butter
1 tablespoon cinnamon
½ cup honey
1 cup buttermilk
1 ounce fresh yeast (or 2 packages dry yeast, proofed; see p. 8)
¼ cup cool water
2 cups whole wheat flour
3-3½ cups unbleached all-purpose white flour
1½ cups raisins

Pour the boiling water over the salt, oats, and butter in a large bowl. Stir with a large wire whisk until the butter is melted. Then let the mixture stand for a few minutes. (Most of the liquid will be absorbed.) Sprinkle on the cinnamon and blend it in gradually to avoid lumping. Stir in the buttermilk and the honey. Allow the mixture to cool to room temperature. Meanwhile, dissolve the yeast in the cool water and let it stand for 5 minutes. Then add the yeast to the liquid mixture in the bowl. Beat in the whole wheat flour. Stir in 2 cups of the white flour, using a wooden spoon in place of the whisk, which would become clogged by the thick dough.

Following the instructions for dislodging the dough from the bowl in the White Bread recipe, sprinkle ½ cup flour around the edge of the dough and work the flour underneath it with a wooden spoon. Rub ¼ cup flour onto your kneading cloth. Turn the dough out of the bowl onto the cloth and sprinkle it with ¼ cup additional flour. Work the dough into one homogenous mass by turning it over and over on the floured cloth, lifting it gently with the sides of your hands (prekneading). Then knead the dough for about 5 minutes, using the amount necessary of the remaining ½ cup of flour.

Allow the dough 2 rises in an oiled bowl. Each rise will take about an hour. Knead the dough for about 3 to 5 minutes between the rises. After the second rise, knead in the raisins, a handful at a time, to distribute them evenly. Cut the dough in half. Form each half into a smooth ball and place each in a greased and floured loaf pan. Allow the dough to rise a third time until doubled in bulk. (This bread will not triple in bulk, because the oats do not rise at all and whole wheat flour is heavy.)

Glaze the risen breads with melted butter, and bake them in a preheated 350-degree oven for 40 to 45 minutes. To test for doneness, a toothpick inserted into the middle of the loaf should come out bone dry. (If, during the baking, the loaves brown too quickly, lightly lay a piece of aluminum foil over them.)

Immediately upon removing the breads from the oven, turn them out of the pans onto wire racks. Allow them to cool for 2 to 3 hours before eating or wrapping.

QUICK BREADS

In a book otherwise devoted to long-rising yeast breads, here is a chapter on breads that you can prepare for the oven or steamer in a matter of minutes. The leavening agents used are baking powder and baking soda, which act almost immediately.

There are literally hundreds of varieties of quick breads. This short chapter covers the major kinds in their basic form, and the recipes are just waiting for your own additions and innovations. Once you learn the textures of the different doughs and batters, and when to use baking powder or soda, you will hardly need to follow a recipe at all.

Baking powder and baking soda both work by neutralization reactions, releasing carbon dioxide gas. This gas gets entrapped in a dough or batter as bubbles, causing the dough to expand. Baking powder is an acid substance; it takes an alkaline substance, such as milk (often referred to as "sweet" milk), to neutralize it. Baking soda is an alkaline substance and requires an acid, such as buttermilk, yogurt, or sour cream, to neutralize it.

Acid milks, besides neutralizing baking soda, have another important attribute: they have a tenderizing effect on quick doughs and batters. (In yeast breads, this tenderizing effect is minimal. The acid milks will give yeast breads a fine tangy flavor, but the yeast, not the acid milk, breaks down the grain.) This is a very important fact to take into consideration when you want to bake quick breads with whole-grain flours. Whole-grain quick breads made with "sweet" milk tend to be tough and to have a texture like bird seed. The same bread made with an acid milk is delightfully tender and delicious.

You will notice that the "sweet" milk recipes use baking powder exclusively. Some of the acid milk recipes use baking soda alone, but others use it in conjunction with baking powder. The reason for using both is that modern "double-acting" baking powders are stronger leavening agents than soda; thus, the soda is used to neutralize the acid milk, and then the powder takes over to finish off the rising process.

Baking Powder Biscuits

This biscuit recipe contains more milk than most, thus producing extremely light, feathery biscuits.

**2 cups unbleached, all-purpose
   white flour**
**4 teaspoons double-acting
   baking powder**
½ teaspoon salt
**4-6 tablespoons butter, softened to
   room temperature**
⅞ cup cold "sweet" milk

Mix the flour, baking powder, and salt in a mixing bowl. Cut the butter into the flour, using a pastry blender, until the mixture resembles cornmeal. (If you do not have a pastry blender, rub the butter into the flour with your hands.)

Add the milk all at once, blending it in with a wooden spoon or a rubber spatula. Allow the dough to stand in the bowl for about a minute, so that the flour can thoroughly absorb the milk. Turn the dough out onto a well-floured pastry cloth or wooden board. Sprinkle the dough with a teaspoon or two of additional flour and knead it gently and briefly (about 30 seconds).

Roll or pat the dough to a thickness of about ½ inch. Be sure to keep your rolling pin and cloth or board well floured so that this soft dough does not stick. Cut out biscuits with a floured cutter or a knife and place them on a greased and floured baking sheet. Chill the biscuits for at least 15 minutes or for as long as 4 hours before baking.

About 15 minutes before baking, preheat the oven to 450 degrees and place the oven rack to the highest position. Bake the biscuits for 10 to 12 minutes, until very lightly browned. Serve piping hot.

VARIATIONS

SPIRAL BISCUITS: Roll the dough about ¼ inch thick and brush it with 2 or 3 tablespoons of cooled, melted butter, leaving a ½-inch border at one end. Sprinkle cinnamon-sugar and nuts, if desired, on top of the butter. Moisten the ½-inch border with cold water (using your fingers) and roll up the dough, toward the border, like a jelly roll. The water or milk will seal the roll. Cut off ¾-inch slices and place them, cut side down, on the baking sheet. Proceed as directed above.

BUTTERMILK BISCUITS: Reduce the baking powder to 2 teaspoons and add 1 teaspoon of baking soda. (Crush the soda with a spoon to eliminate lumps.) Substitute buttermilk for the "sweet" milk and then proceed as directed above.

WHOLE WHEAT BUTTERMILK BISCUITS: Substitute 1 cup of whole wheat flour for 1 cup of white flour. Reduce the baking powder

to 2 teaspoons and add 1 teaspoon of baking soda. Substitute buttermilk for "sweet" milk, and then proceed as directed above.

DROP BISCUITS: Use the "sweet" milk, buttermilk, or whole wheat variations. Increase the milk or buttermilk to 1⅓ cups. This dough is too moist to be kneaded. It is dropped (using 2 spoons) into greased and floured muffin cups or on top of a cobbler or chicken pie mixture. Drop biscuits are baked at 425 degrees for 15 to 20 minutes in the middle level of the oven.

An important rule to follow for cobblers or chicken pie: the cobbler or pie mixture must be bubbling hot before you drop on the biscuit mixture, and then it is immediately replaced in the 425-degree oven for baking.

Corn Bread

Yield: One 8-inch square or 9-inch round bread, or 12 2¾-inch muffins

Corn bread is a perfect accompaniment for chili con carne, fried chicken, or even scrambled eggs. It is incredibly easy to make. The dry ingredients are mixed in one bowl, the wet ones in another, and then the two are gently combined and baked.

1½ cups stone-ground yellow cornmeal
½ cup unbleached, all-purpose white flour
4 teaspoons double-acting baking powder
½ teaspoon salt
1 egg
⅓ cup honey
¼ cup melted butter, cooled
⅔ cup milk

Grease and flour an 8-inch square or 9-inch round pan or 12 muffin cups. Preheat the oven to 375 degrees. Set the oven rack in the middle position. Combine the cornmeal, flour, baking powder, and salt in a large bowl. Beat the egg with the honey in another bowl and add the butter and the milk. Pour the wet ingredients into the dry ones and stir to blend well. Do not beat. Pour the batter into the prepared pan or muffin cups and bake the bread for 20 to 25 minutes and the muffins for about 15 minutes. A toothpick inserted in the middle will come out dry. Serve hot.

Blueberry Muffins

I bake muffins, pancakes, and waffles often for breakfast, and feel that I am giving my family and guests a good start to the day if I use whole wheat flour. These baked products taste every bit as tender and delicious as the less nutritious ones made with white flour, because buttermilk, yogurt, or sour cream is used to tenderize the batters (see page 51).

1 cup stone-ground
   whole wheat flour
1½ teaspoons baking soda
½ teaspoon cinnamon
1 cup fresh, frozen, or drained
   canned blueberries
1 egg
¼ cup honey
1 tablespoon oil or melted butter
½ teaspoon vanilla
½ cup thick plain yogurt or sour
   cream or scant ½ cup buttermilk

Grease and flour the muffin cups. Preheat the oven to 375 degrees and set the oven rack in the middle position.

Combine the whole wheat flour, baking soda, and cinnamon in the bowl. Be sure to crush the soda with a spoon to eliminate lumps. Stir in the blueberries.

In another bowl, beat the egg with the honey and oil or butter. Add the vanilla and yogurt, sour cream, or buttermilk. Beat well. Then pour the liquids over the dry flour-and-blueberry mixture and stir gently to combine. Do not beat. Divide the mixture evenly among the 8 muffin cups and bake 15 to 18 minutes, or until a toothpick inserted comes out dry. Serve hot.

VARIATIONS

APPLE MUFFINS: Substitute 1 large grated McIntosh or Cortland apple for the blueberries. Increase the cinnamon to ¾ teaspoon and add a dash of nutmeg or allspice, if desired.

BANANA MUFFINS: Omit the cinnamon. Substitute 2 medium-size mashed bananas (1 cup of pulp) for the blueberries. The bananas should be very ripe. Add 1 or 2 drops almond extract, if desired.

CARROT-RAISIN-SPICE MUFFINS: Omit the vanilla. Substitute 1 cup grated raw carrot for the blueberries. Add ¼ teaspoon each of ginger and allspice. Add ⅓ cup raisins with the dry ingredients.

YAM OR WINTER SQUASH MUFFINS: Substitute 1 cup mashed yams, butternut squash, or Hubbard squash for the blueberries. Increase the cinnamon to ¾ teaspoon, and add ¼ teaspoon each ginger and allspice, if desired. Add ⅓ cup broken walnuts or pecans with the dry ingredients.

Steamed Boston Brown Bread

Yield: One loaf

Boston brown bread is the perfect partner for homemade baked beans. Its deep, robust flavor comes from three whole-grain flours and molasses. Its moist, appealing texture is the result of steaming the bread rather than baking it. If you have never steamed a bread before, you will find complete instructions below. You may even find yourself steaming banana breads, cranberry breads, and date-nut breads. Any recipe for a 9-by-5-inch quick bread loaf will fit into two 1-pound coffee cans.

½ cup stone-ground
  whole wheat flour
½ cup stone-ground rye flour
½ cup stone-ground
  yellow cornmeal
1 teaspoon baking soda
½ teaspoon salt
½ cup raisins (or cut-up figs,
  dates, or nuts)
⅜ cup molasses
1 cup buttermilk

Put a large soup kettle, containing about 3 inches of water, on top of the stove to boil. Also have a teapot or other small pot full of boiling water on the stove, so that you can add more water to the kettle as needed. Grease a 1-pound coffee can very well. (There is no need to flour it.) Prepare a double layer of aluminum foil to cover the coffee can, and grease the foil where it will be covering the batter. Have a long length of string ready to tie the foil onto the can.

Mix the whole wheat flour, rye flour, cornmeal, baking soda, and salt in a mixing bowl. (Be sure to crush the lumps out of the soda with a spoon.) Stir in the raisins.

Combine the molasses and buttermilk in a 2-cup measure or a small bowl. Pour this onto the flour mixture, and stir to moisten all the dry ingredients. Do not beat. Pour the batter into the prepared coffee can. Cover the can with the foil and tie the foil on securely with the string. Place the can in the kettle of boiling water. Add more boiling water, if necessary, so that the water comes halfway up the can. Maintain the water level throughout the steaming. Cover the kettle. Steam the bread for 2¼ hours; a toothpick inserted in the middle will come out dry. (Breads take much longer to steam than to bake, because steaming temperature is only 212 degrees.)

When the bread is done, unmold it from its can onto a rack and serve it hot, warm, or cold.

NOTE: You may steam as many cans at the same time as will fit comfortably in your kettle.

Date-Nut Bread

Yield: One 9-by-5-inch loaf

This bread is delightful served slightly warm for breakfast or for tea, with butter. It is also delicious when cold, served with cream cheese.

1¼ cups stone-ground
  whole wheat flour
1¼ cups unbleached, all-purpose
  white flour
2 teaspoons baking powder
1 teaspoon baking soda
1 teaspoon salt
1 cup broken walnuts or pecans
⅓ cup boiling water
1 cup chopped dates
1 egg
½ cup unsulphured molasses
⅓ cup dark brown sugar
½ cup thick sour cream
4 tablespoons butter, melted

Grease and flour a 9-by-5-inch loaf pan. Preheat the oven to 325 degrees, with the oven rack placed in the middle position.

Mix the whole wheat flour, white flour, the baking powder and soda, and salt in a large mixing bowl. (Crush the soda with a spoon to eliminate any lumps.) Stir in the nuts.

Pour the boiling water on the dates in another bowl and allow them to stand for 5 minutes. Then beat in the egg, molasses, brown sugar, sour cream, and butter. Pour this liquid-and-date mixture over the dry ingredients and stir gently to combine. Do not beat. Transfer the batter to the prepared loaf pan and bake the bread for about 60 to 65 minutes, or until a toothpick inserted in the center of the loaf comes out dry. Do not worry if the top of the loaf is cracked; this is normal.

Remove the bread from the oven and allow it to stand in its pan for 15 minutes before turning it out. Then let it cool on a wire rack.

ADVANCED TECHNIQUES

Brioche

A well-made brioche is a light, buttery, airy bread that is made golden yellow with egg yolks. Traditionally, it is baked in a round, fluted mold and has an oval topknot *(brioche à tête)*, or it can be baked as a rectangular loaf divided into sections *(pain brioché)*. After making a few batches of brioche, you may find yourself content and satisfied with this ethereal bread, but don't stop here! You are now at the perfect starting point to try your hand at fancy yeast breads and cakes, because virtually all of them (croissants, Danish, stollen, babka, savarin, etc.) are based on a brioche dough.

Brioche will take about six to seven hours from start to finish; about eight to nine hours from the beginning to the point when you can eat them. If you wish to distribute the work over several days, rather than devoting one whole day to making the dough, see the section on "Slowing Up a Yeast Dough." The 5½ cups of flour in each recipe will produce two large breads, baked in either round, fluted molds that measure approximately 8 inches across the top or in 9-by-5-inch loaf pans. Each recipe will also yield about 36 roll-sized brioches.

There are three basic formulas for brioche dough. They are all made in exactly the same way; they differ from one another only in their relative richness.

Brioche I

The least rich, although absolutely delicious and well suited for simple brioche loaves or rolls.

1 cup milk
4 tablespoons sweet butter
2 teaspoons salt
1 cup hot mashed potatoes
  (1 medium-sized potato)
½ cup honey
4 egg yolks
1 ounce fresh yeast (or 2 packages
  dry yeast, proofed; see p. 8)
¼ cup cool water
5-5½ cups unbleached
  all-purpose flour

Brioche II

The richest dough, which makes extraordinary brioche loaves or rolls, but which is especially suited for turning into babkas (coffee cakes).

1 cup milk
8 tablespoons (1 stick) sweet butter
1 tablespoon salt
1 cup hot mashed potatoes
  (1 medium-sized potato)
½ cup honey
8 egg yolks
1½ ounces fresh yeast (or 3 packages
  dry yeast, proofed; see p. 8)
¼ cup cool water
5-5½ cups unbleached
  all-purpose flour

Brioche III

This dough is rich in butter and egg yolks, but it is less sweet than the preceding formulas. Use this as a wrap for a coulibiac of salmon, a beef Wellington, or a pâté en croûte. If you prefer less sweet bread, this makes perfect brioche loaves and rolls as well.

1 cup milk
8 tablespoons (1 stick) sweet butter
1 tablespoon salt
1 cup hot mashed potatoes
   (1 medium-sized potato)
¼ cup honey
8 egg yolks
1 ounce fresh yeast (or 2 packages
   dry yeast, proofed; see p. 8)
¼ cup cool water
5-5½ cups unbleached
   all-purpose flour

Heat ½ cup of the milk to scalding and pour it over the butter and salt in a large bowl. Add the hot mashed potatoes, blending them in with a large wire whisk or wooden spoon. When the butter is melted, add the rest of the milk, the honey, and the egg yolks. Allow the mixture to cool to about room temperature. Meanwhile, dissolve the yeast in the cool water and let it stand for 5 minutes. Then add the yeast to the liquid mixture in the bowl. Beat in 4 cups of the flour, 1 cup at a time. If you are using a whisk, switch to a spoon after 2 or 3 cups, because the whisk will get clogged.

Although the dough may seem terribly soft at this stage, it is time to turn it out of the bowl, because the softer the dough, the more fluffy your finished brioche will be.

Have another 1½ cups flour ready to use as follows: Sprinkle ½ cup flour around the edge of the dough and another ¼ cup flour onto your kneading cloth. Rub the flour into the cloth. With a wooden spoon, work the flour underneath the dough, by moving your spoon in downward strokes around the sides of the bowl. Turn the bowl over, and the dough will fall out onto your floured kneading surface. Sprinkle ¼ cup flour over dough and work it into one homogeneous mass by turning it over and over on the floured cloth, lifting it gently with the sides of your hands. The dough is very soft and sticky, so be sure not to put your fingers into it, for they will get stuck. In a minute or so, the dough will feel less sticky and you can start to knead heartily.

One half cup of flour is left. Use it, a little at a time, to flour the cloth each time the dough seems to be getting sticky. Turn the dough around on the floured cloth to lightly powder its surface. To knead, push and stretch the dough from the center outwards, with the heels of your hands; flip the dough in half and quickly flip the whole mass over. Repeat this process for about 5 minutes, flouring the cloth as necessary, then rolling the dough around on the floured cloth.

The Rising of the Dough: First and Second Rises

After kneading for about 5 minutes, you will notice that the dough feels springy and pops back at you when you press it with your finger. Place the dough in a well-oiled bowl. Turn the dough in the bowl so that it becomes lightly filmed with the oil. Cover the bowl with a damp towel. Place it to rise in a draft-free place, at room temperature, until the dough almost doubles in bulk (approximately 1½ hours).

After this first rise, punch the dough down in the bowl and turn it out onto your floured kneading surface. Knead it for another 5 minutes. Re-oil the bowl if necessary, replace the dough in it, turn the dough to lightly oil its surface, and allow it to rise a second time (approximately 1¼ hours, or until almost doubled in bulk).

After the dough has risen for the second time, punch it down, turn it out onto your floured kneading surface, and knead it for a few minutes. With a sharp knife, cut the dough in half to make 2 loaves. Grease the baking pans thoroughly, using solid vegetable shortening, and then sprinkle in some flour. Knock the flour about to make an even coating and then knock out the excess.

The Shaping of the Dough and the Third Rise

To shape the brioche *à tête*, take the dough for 1 loaf and divide it into a large piece for the base and a small piece for the head. Knead the large piece into a smooth ball and place it in the prepared pan. Cut a cross in the top with a pair of scissors. Knead the small piece into an oval shape and insert the small end into the incision, pressing it well into the large ball. Roll-sized brioche are shaped in exactly the same way. The dough is divided into roll-sized portions (about 36 for the entire recipe), and a small piece is cut from each to make the oval-shaped head. If you do not have the traditional roll-sized fluted molds, use greased and floured muffin tins.

To shape a *pain brioché* in a 9-by-5-inch loaf pan, simply divide the dough for 1 loaf into 3 equal pieces. Knead each into a smooth ball and place them next to each other in the prepared pan.

Cover the shaped dough with a damp dish towel and let the breads rise until they are approximately triple in bulk (rising time about 1½ to 2 hours).

Glazing and Baking the Brioche

For large brioches, preheat the oven to 325 degrees and set the oven rung in the lowest position. For roll-sized brioches, preheat the oven to 375 degrees and set the oven rung in the highest position. Glaze the risen loaves or rolls with 1 egg beaten with 2 tablespoons of water. Place in the oven. Bake rolls 10 to 15 minutes or until nicely browned. A large round brioche will bake in approximately 45 minutes. Large 9-by-5-inch loaves will bake in approximately 30 minutes. To test large breads for doneness, tap the loaves; they should sound hollow. Also, a toothpick inserted into the fattest part of the loaf should come out bone dry.

Immediately upon removing the breads from the oven, turn them out of the pans onto wire racks. Rolls may be eaten warm, but the loaves must cool for 2 to 3 hours before eating. In any case, do not wrap any bread until it is completely cooled.

Savarin, Babas au Rhum, Kugelhopf

Savarin, babas, and Kugelhopf are all yeast cakes made from a batterlike dough. The dough is similar to brioche, except that not enough flour is added for the dough to be kneaded. Instead, it is beaten in the bowl with a wooden spoon for three or four minutes, which, by the way, is very good exercise indeed. These batter-doughs require only two rises, rather than the three given to kneaded yeast doughs. First the dough rises in its mixing bowl, then, after it has been thoroughly beaten down, it is spooned into its mold (or molds) and rises for a second and final time. Because these doughs do not have the firmness of a kneaded dough, they must not be allowed to rise more than double; otherwise, they will collapse.

A savarin is baked in a ring mold, in this case one with a 6½-to-7½-cup capacity, and babas are baked in small cup-shaped molds that measure about 2½ inches in diameter as well as in height. After the cakes are baked and unmolded, they are cooled briefly, and then soaked with a rum syrup. A Kugelhopf is baked in a fancy, fluted, deep tube mold that has a capacity of 9 or 10 cups. When the batter is spooned into the mold, it is alternated with layers of raisins, nuts, or chocolate and sprinklings of cinnamon-sugar. It is not soaked with syrup.

The recipe that follows is a rather small one, producing one savarin, one dozen babas, or one Kugelhopf. I always find myself doubling the recipe and producing a combination of cakes. However, I realize that most people want only one cake at a time; hence the small recipe. (This dough would be a little tricky to freeze. Because it is so soft, you would have to freeze it in a bowl, rather than a plastic bag. This would take up more freezer space and remove one of your mixing bowls from active use.) For additional ideas for Kugelhopf dough ingredients, please see pages 67 to 72.

THE DOUGH

4 tablespoons butter, melted
¼-⅓ cup hot mashed potato
(1 small potato)
¼ cup honey
3 egg yolks
¾ teaspoon salt
½ cup milk
¾ teaspoon vanilla extract
¾ ounce fresh yeast (or 1½ packages
dry yeast, proofed; see p. 8)
2 tablespoons cool water
2¼ cups unbleached,
all-purpose white flour

Combine the melted butter and mashed potato in a mixing bowl. Then blend in the honey, egg yolks, salt, milk, and vanilla. (The mixture should be about room temperature. If it is hotter, let it cool.)

Dissolve the yeast in the cool water and let it stand for 5 minutes. Then add the yeast mixture to the liquid mixture in the bowl. Beat in the flour, ½ cup at a time, and when all the flour is added, continue beating with a wooden spoon for 3 or 4 minutes. This will activate the gluten in the flour and takes the place of kneading.

Scrape down the sides of the bowl with a rubber spatula and cover the bowl with plastic wrap or a dampened cloth. Allow the dough to rise until doubled in bulk at room temperature (about 1 to 1½ hours). When the dough is risen, beat it down with a wooden spoon and continue to beat it for 2 or 3 minutes. Now you are ready to spoon the dough into its mold or molds, following the directions for the specific cake you wish to bake.

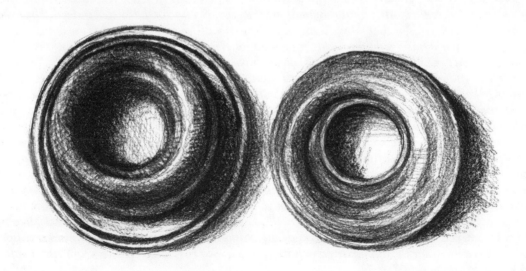

Savarin

1 recipe dough, p. 62

Grease the ring mold with solid vegetable shortening, and sprinkle it with a few tablespoons of flour. Knock the flour about to coat the mold evenly, and then knock out the excess.

Spoon the dough into the ring mold, turning the mold as you proceed, so that the dough is fairly evenly distributed. Do not worry that it is not spread smoothly; it will shape up perfectly as it rises. The mold should be about half full. Allow the dough to rise, uncovered, until it is doubled in bulk; in other words, it will fill the mold. This will take about 1 to 1½ hours. The reason the dough is uncovered is that it is very soft and would inevitably stick to a cloth or plastic wrap. While the dough is rising this second time, prepare the rum syrup below. The syrup should be about lukewarm when used; it may be made ahead and reheated.

Just before you decide that the dough has doubled, preheat the oven to 350 degrees and arrange the oven rack in the lowest position. Bake the savarin for about 25 minutes, or until a toothpick inserted into its middle comes out dry. (If the savarin starts browning too soon during the baking, lightly lay a piece of aluminum foil over it.)

Remove the savarin from the oven, and let it stand in its pan for 5 minutes before unmolding. Then reverse the cake onto a wire rack, remove the pan, and let the cake cool for about ½ hour before you soak it in the syrup.

Soaking the Savarin

Just before soaking, poke holes all over the cake with a toothpick — top, bottom, outside and inside. This will facilitate the cake's absorption of the syrup. Place the cake, rounded side down, on its serving platter and gradually spoon on a few tablespoons of syrup. Tilt the platter so that you can spoon some more of the syrup onto the outside and inside circumference of the ring. Now turn the cake over again so that the rounded side is up. This is the side you will leave up for serving. Spoon some more of the syrup over the rounded side, and again tilt the platter so that more syrup can be spooned inside and outside. The cake should be quite moist, but not soggy. You will probably not use all the syrup. Store the remainder in a

tightly covered jar for future use. You can let the cake sit in a small puddle of syrup on its platter for about an hour, but carefully drain off the excess before serving.

Decorating and Serving the Savarin

After draining the excess syrup from the platter, you can glaze the savarin with a few spoonfuls of apricot jam that have been melted with a tablespoon of dark rum. You can then affix sliced nuts and/or candied fruits to the glaze and pass around a bowl of lightly sweetened whipped cream or custard sauce as you serve the cake.

In the summertime, it is lovely to fill the center of the ring with fresh, slightly sweetened berries and to pipe a decorative design of whipped cream around and on the cake. Pass more whipped cream in a bowl.

Babas au Rhum

Yield: Twelve babas 2½ inches wide and 2½ inches deep

1 recipe dough, p. 62

Grease the baba molds with solid vegetable shortening and sprinkle each with flour. Knock the flour about to coat the molds evenly, and then knock out the excess.

Spoon the dough into the molds, filling them between one-third and half full. Set the molds on a baking sheet, and allow them to rise, uncovered, at room temperature until doubled in bulk; the rounded top of each risen baba will just be peeking over the rim of its mold. Rising will take about 45 minutes to 1 hour. The reason the dough is kept uncovered is that it is very soft and would stick to a cloth or plastic wrap. While the dough is rising this second time, prepare the rum syrup below. The syrup should be about lukewarm when used; it may be made ahead and reheated.

Just before you decide that the dough is doubled, preheat the oven to 375 degrees and place the oven rack in the middle position. Bake the babas (on their baking sheet) for about 15 minutes, or until a toothpick inserted comes out dry. If they start to brown too much while baking, cover them lightly with a sheet of aluminum foil.

Remove the babas from the oven and unmold them. Let them cool, on a wire rack standing upright, for 15 to 20 minutes before soaking them in the syrup.

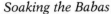

Soaking the Babas

Just before soaking, poke holes all over the babas with a toothpick — top, bottom, and sides. Place the babas upside down in a large serving dish. (An oblong pyrex dish or large glass pie pans are good if you do not have a fancy large platter with sides.) Spoon some syrup gradually over the cakes. Turn them upright and spoon on a bit more. Now lay the babas on their sides and spoon on more syrup, rolling them around occasionally. Babas can soak up more syrup than a savarin made out of the same amount of dough because there are more exposed sides. The babas should become quite moist but not soggy. It is possible that you may not use all the syrup. Store the remainder in a tightly covered jar for future use. You can let the babas sit in a very shallow puddle of syrup for about 15 minutes after pouring, but then carefully drain off most of the excess. Use a bulb baster or a gravy spoon to help remove the extra syrup.

Glazing and Serving the Babas

After removing the extra syrup from the dish, you can glaze the babas with a few spoonfuls of apricot jam that have been melted with a tablespoon of dark rum.

Babas are usually served as is, but they are delightful served with lightly sweetened whipped cream and fresh berries.

Rum Syrup

This syrup could easily be flavored with other spirits, such as bourbon, Kirsch, or Grand Marnier. Then you would simply have to change the name of your cakes to Babas au Bourbon, etc. The completely cooled syrup can be stored indefinitely in a tightly covered jar.

¾ cup sugar
1 cup water
¼ cup dark rum

Bring the sugar and water to a boil in a saucepan without stirring. Reduce the heat to a simmer, cover the pan, and allow the syrup to simmer for 1 minute. Uncover the pan and remove it from the heat. Stir the syrup to cool it slightly for 1 minute, then stir in the rum.

Kugelhopf

1 recipe dough, p. 62
1 cup raisins, nuts, or chocolate
   chips (or a combination)
¼ cup sugar mixed with
   1 teaspoon cinnamon

Grease a 9- or 10-cup Kugelhopf mold very well with solid vegetable shortening. Be sure that you have greased inside all the flutes and decorations. Sprinkle the mold with a few tablespoons of flour. Knock the flour about to coat the mold evenly, and then knock out the excess.

Spoon a small amount of dough into the bottom of the mold, spreading it out with the back of the spoon. Sprinkle on some of the raisins, nuts, or chocolate. Press them into the dough. Sprinkle on some of the cinnamon-sugar. Continue layering until all the ingredients are used up. The top layer should be dough.

Allow the dough to rise at room temperature, uncovered, until it is just doubled in bulk. (It will barely fill the pan when risen.) The reason the dough is left uncovered is that it is very soft and would stick to a cloth or plastic wrap.

Just before you decide the dough is doubled, preheat the oven to 350 degrees and place the oven rack in the lowest position. Bake the Kugelhopf for 30 to 35 minutes, or until a toothpick inserted into the fattest part comes out dry. If you have used chocolate, be careful not to confuse melted chocolate on the toothpick with uncooked dough. The chocolate will always look wet.

Remove the cake from the oven and allow it to cool for 5 minutes in its pan. Then reverse it onto a wire rack, and remove the pan. The cake is left upside down to show off the pretty design of the mold. Allow it to cool for 2 or 3 hours before eating or wrapping. You may sprinkle it lightly with powdered sugar before serving.

Babkas

Babkas are yeast coffee cakes that are filled with dried, cooked or fresh fruits, nuts, streusel, or chocolate. Babkas can be shaped into braids, loaves, rings, round discs for Kuchen, or little rolls. Any moderately sweet yeast dough can be used as the base for a babka. The Brioche II recipe on page 58 is excellent for this use. Somewhat different in taste is the following sour cream yeast dough, which is slightly heavier and moister than the brioche. Please note the variations in flavorings that directly follow the sour cream babka dough; they can be used with the brioche recipe as well. This dough freezes perfectly, so I have given you a rather large recipe. You might want to use half and freeze half. Once you have all your utensils and the kitchen ready for a yeast dough, it is really worthwhile to make a large batch.

THE SOUR CREAM DOUGH

Yield: 2 large cakes or 24 roll-sized cakes

8 tablespoons (½ cup) sweet butter, melted
¾ cup hot mashed potatoes (1 medium-small potato)
2 teaspoons salt
½ cup honey
½ pint (1 cup) sour cream
6 egg yolks
1½ teaspoons vanilla
1½ ounces fresh yeast (or 3 packages dry yeast, proofed; see p. 8)
¼ cup cool water
5-5½ cups unbleached, all-purpose white flour

Combine the butter and potatoes in a large mixing bowl, using a large wire whisk. Blend in the salt, honey, sour cream, egg yolks, and vanilla. The mixture should be at about room temperature. Dissolve the yeast in the cool water and let it stand for 5 minutes. Then add it to the liquid mixture in the bowl. Stir in 4 cups of the flour, 1 cup at a time. Switch from the whisk to a large wooden spoon after 2 or 3 cups, because the whisk will get clogged.

Following the instructions for dislodging the dough from the bowl in the White Bread recipe, sprinkle ¼ cup flour around the edge of the dough and work the flour underneath it with a wooden spoon. Rub ¼ cup flour onto your kneading cloth. Turn the dough out of the bowl onto the cloth and sprinkle it with ¼ cup additional flour. Work the dough into one homogeneous mass by turning it over and over on the floured cloth, lifting it gently with the sides of your hands (prekneading). Then knead the dough for about 5 minutes, using only as much as necessary of the remaining ¾ cup of flour.

Allow the dough 2 rises in an oiled bowl. Each rise will take about 1½ hours. Knead the dough for 3 to 5 minutes after each rise. Then fill and shape the babka, following one of the methods described on the following page.

Flavoring Variations

1. Add the finely grated rind of 2 oranges or 2 lemons (or one of each) within the vanilla.

2. Add 2 tablespoons of Grand Marnier, dark rum, Cognac, or Amaretto with the vanilla.

3. Add 1 tablespoon of ground cinnamon, or a mixture of cinnamon, nutmeg, allspice, and ginger, with the potatoes. (Adding the spices while the mixture is still thick avoids any tendency to lumping.)

Large Streusel-Filled Babka Braid

Yield: 10-12 servings

½ recipe sour cream dough or
½ recipe Brioche II

STREUSEL INGREDIENTS:

10 tablespoons sweet butter,
softened to room temperature
1¼ cups firmly packed brown sugar
1¼ cups flour
2½ teaspoons cinnamon
Pinch of salt
1 cup walnuts, pecans, chocolate
chips, raisins, or other dried fruit,
cut small

FOR THE GLAZE:

2 tablespoons additional butter,
melted and cooled

Bake the braid on an 11-by-15-inch jelly-roll pan.

After the dough has risen for the second time, knead it on the pastry cloth for 3 to 5 minutes. Then divide the dough into 3 fairly even pieces. Flour the cut edges well to avoid sticking and cover the dough with a cloth. Allow the dough to rest for 15 to 20 minutes before attempting to roll it out. (After kneading the dough, the gluten is quite active, and the dough is nearly impossible to roll thin with a pin. The thinner you roll a dough that you want to fill, the more surface area you will have for the filling; thus the rest period.) While the dough is resting, prepare the streusel filling and the jelly-roll pan.

To prepare the streusel, combine the butter, brown sugar, flour, cinnamon, and salt in a mixing bowl. Mix all the ingredients together until they become crumbly, using your fingers or a wooden spoon. Reserve ¼ cup of this streusel to sprinkle over the top of the finished braid. Divide the rest into 3 fairly even parts. (Streusel can be made 2 to 3 days ahead of time and kept refrigerated. Just let it come to room temperature before you use it, because it tends to become a solid block when cold.)

To prepare the jelly-roll pan, grease it well with solid vegetable shortening. Attach an aluminum foil border on each long side of the pan with a large overhang, which will be used to protect the cake edges during the baking. Grease the foil border well (but not the overhang). Then flour the pan and the border. Knock out the excess.

Shaping the Braid

Roll one piece of the rested dough into a large rectangle about 11 by 17 inches. Flour the cloth and turn the dough over as necessary to prevent sticking. The shape will not be exact, and the measurements are only estimates. It will even out in the end. Spread one-third of the streusel evenly on the dough, leaving one long edge (17 inches) empty for a width of about 1 inch. The other 3 edges should be as well covered with the streusel as the center, so that the finished babka will be evenly filled. Now sprinkle on top of the streusel ⅓ cup of your choice of dried fruit, nuts, or chocolate. Press the pieces into the dough with your fingers so that they do not fall out as you roll out the dough.

Lightly moisten the empty edge with cold water, using your fingers or a pastry brush. Starting at the other long edge, roll up the dough like a jelly roll, rolling very tightly. There should be no air spaces inside your roll. When you have finished rolling, press the roll firmly on the cloth, with the moistened edge on the bottom. This will glue your roll closed. Set this roll aside, and repeat with the other 2 pieces of rested dough and the remainder of the filling ingredients.

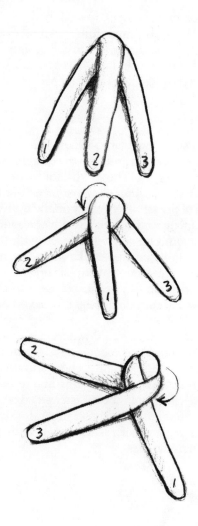

Arrange the 3 rolls on the kneading cloth, facing you, with the longest one in the center. Place the tops of the 2 outside rolls underneath the middle one and pull the top of the middle roll gently over them and underneath to seal the 3 rolls together. Now you are ready to braid. Simply pull an outside roll over the center roll, and then the opposite outside roll over the new center roll. Notice that each roll becomes the next center roll as it is pulled over. These rolls are fat and a bit cumbersome, but they will form a handsome, chubby braid. When you come to the end, seal the bottom just as you did the top; pull the center roll gently over and underneath the others.

Carefully pick up the braid by the ends, slightly compressing it with your hands as you do, and place it on the prepared baking sheet. Cover it with a dry cloth. Allow the dough to rise to 2½ times its original bulk, which will take about 1½ to 2 hours.

Preheat the oven to 325 degrees and place the oven rack on the second shelf from the bottom. Glaze the risen dough with the melted butter and sprinkle it with the reserved streusel. Loosely cover the braid with the foil overhang. (It should not press on the dough.) Cover the ends of the braid with additional pieces of foil. Do not cover the middle of the cake. Fold back the edges of the foil overhang if they are so long that they cover the middle of the cake. All this foil will keep the edges of the babka from drying out while the center cooks. The cake will take 1 to 1¼ hours to bake. Uncover the cake during the last part of the baking to brown it lightly. A toothpick inserted near the center of the cake should come out with no dough adhering to it. (Be careful that you do not mistake melted chocolate or soft streusel for dough.)

Remove the cake from the oven, and using 2 flat, wide utensils, lift the cake from the baking pan and place it on a large wire rack to cool. The utensils could be long, wide spatulas, flat pot covers, the bottom discs from springform pans, etc. Make use of what you have in your kitchen.

Cool the cake 2 to 3 hours before eating or wrapping it.

Kugelhopf or Bundtkuchen Made with Sour Cream Babka Dough

Yield: One round cake serving 6-8

See page 66 for another Kugelhopf recipe.

REVISED SOUR CREAM DOUGH:

4 tablespoons (¼ cup) sweet butter, melted

¼-⅓ cup hot mashed potatoes (1 small potato)

1 teaspoon salt

¼ cup honey

½ cup sour cream

3 egg yolks

¾ teaspoon vanilla

Half the amount of any flavoring variation for babka dough on p. 68, optional

¾ ounce fresh yeast (or 1½ packages dry yeast, proofed; see p. 8)

2 tablespoons cool water

2¼ cups unbleached, all-purpose white flour

FILLING INGREDIENTS:

1 cup raisins, nuts, or chocolate chips (or a combination)

¼ cup sugar mixed with 1 teaspoon cinnamon

Bake the cake in a decorative 10-cup tube cake pan.

Combine the butter and potatoes in a mixing bowl. Then blend in the salt, honey, sour cream, egg yolks, vanilla, and optional flavoring. The mixture should be about room temperature. If it is hotter, let it cool.

Dissolve the yeast in the cool water and let it stand for 5 minutes. Then add the yeast mixture to the liquid mixture in the bowl. Beat in the flour ½ cup at a time, and when all the flour is added, continue beating with a wooden spoon for 3 or 4 minutes. This will activate the gluten in the flour and takes the place of kneading.

Scrape down the sides of the bowl with a rubber spatula and cover the bowl with plastic wrap or a dampened cloth. Allow the dough to rise until doubled in bulk at room temperature (about 1 to 1½ hours). When the dough is risen, beat it down with a wooden spoon and continue to beat it for 2 or 3 minutes. Now you are ready to spoon the dough into its mold, following the directions for Kugelhopf on page 66. Also follow the directions given there for the second and final rise, baking, and cooling of the cake.

Apple Kuchen

½ recipe sour cream dough or
½ recipe Brioche II
3 pounds McIntosh or Cortland
apples
3 tablespoons orange juice
6 tablespoons sweet butter, melted
and cooled
½ cup sugar mixed with
2 teaspoons cinnamon

After the dough has risen for the second time, knead it on the pastry cloth for 3 to 5 minutes. Divide the dough in half and let it rest for a few minutes while you prepare the baking pans and the apples.

Grease and flour 2 9-inch springform pans. (Springform pans are ideal because they have removable bottoms, which makes removing the baked cakes from the pans very easy. However, you can use two 9-inch round cake pans if you do not have springforms.) Peel, core, and slice the apples about ½ inch thick. Sprinkle them with the orange juice and mix lightly. (The orange juice will reduce discoloration.)

Pat a piece of the rested dough onto the bottom of each pan; it will be quite thin. Brush the dough with some melted butter, about 2 tablespoons per pan, and sprinkle 2 tablespoons of cinnamon-sugar on each as well. Press half the apple slices decoratively onto the dough in each pan, very close together. Brush the apples with the remainder of the melted butter and sprinkle them with the rest of the cinnamon-sugar.

Allow the dough to rise until it is puffing up between the apple slices. It will not quite double. This will take about an hour.

Preheat the oven to 350 degrees. Place the oven rack on the second level from the bottom. Bake the Kuchen for 25 to 30 minutes. A toothpick inserted into a dough part will come out dry. (The fruit will always come out wet on the toothpick — be sure you are testing the dough.)

Remove the cakes from the oven and allow them to stand in their pans for 5 minutes before unmolding. Then unhinge the springs on the springform pans and use a metal spatula to ease them off the pan bottoms onto wire racks to cool. With ordinary cake pans, carefully tilt them out of their pans onto the racks. Use a small knife to free any stuck spots.

The Kuchen may be eaten slightly warm, because the dough part is thin. Allow them to cool for at least 1 hour, however, before serving. They may also be eaten at room temperature.

What Is a Croissant?

A croissant is a crescent-shaped roll that is very buttery, very light, and very flaky. It is made out of a rather complicated dough. It is, in fact, a classic puff pastry made on a yeast dough base. These two different kinds of dough require opposite temperature conditions for optimum results. For puff pastry everything must be kept cold so that the large amount of butter does not ooze out of the dough. When a puff pastry is baked, the ice-cold dough is put into a very hot oven which causes an "explosion" of the butter layers into the flour layers, resulting in a dramatic rise of the pastry. A yeast dough, on the other hand, needs warmth to rise. Cold temperatures cause the yeast to become dormant. To obtain the utmost rising values from both components of a croissant dough, there must therefore be a deliberate balance of hot and cold temperatures. In the recipe that follows, you will notice an almost alternating pattern of warming and then chilling the dough. It is almost like a game: you coax one part and try to "trick" the other. Then you reverse the process.

Making croissants is time-consuming. At the end of the recipe, I have worked out three timetables which will allow you to distribute your work over one, two, or three days. The two- and three-day methods will avoid your staying up all Saturday night to prepare croissants for an elegant Sunday brunch. The one-day method is for night owls and insomniacs. It is also suitable for early risers who want croissants for dinner — heaven forbid.

Twenty-Four Croissants

Because making croissant dough is a rather involved process, I am giving the instructions here in their complete form so that you do not have to flip back and forth between various sections of the book.

Note that the initial ingredients for one batch of croissants are almost exactly half of the ingredients for a batch of Brioche II. The differences are that in croissant dough there is slightly more salt and slightly less yeast.

½ cup milk
2 teaspoons salt
4 tablespoons sweet butter, melted
½ cup hot mashed potatoes
  (1 small potato)
¼ cup honey
4 egg yolks
½ ounce fresh yeast (or 1 package dry
  yeast, proofed; see p. 8)
2 tablespoons cool water
2½ cups unbleached all-purpose
  white flour

THE BUTTER ADDITION:

3 sticks sweet butter
½ cup unbleached all-purpose
  white flour

Combine the milk, salt, butter, and potatoes in a large bowl, using a wire whisk or a wooden spoon. Blend in the honey and the egg yolks. Dissolve the yeast in the cool water in a cup, and let it stand for 5 minutes. Then add it to the mixture in the bowl. (This is a small amount of yeast, so be sure to scrape every bit of it out of the cup.) Stir in 2¼ cups of flour. Sprinkle ¼ cup of flour around the edge of the bowl. Using the wooden spoon, work the flour underneath the dough to help dislodge it from the bowl. Turn the dough out onto a well-floured kneading cloth. Scrape out any dough that has remained in the bowl and add it to the mass on the cloth.

You have ½ cup of flour left from the butter addition. Use the amount necessary (about 2 to 3 tablespoons) for a *very brief kneading* — 1 to 2 minutes. The remainder of this extra ½ cup of flour will be incorporated into the butter, so save it until then.

The dough should be *soft* and *barely handleable*. It is not necessary to knead it thoroughly. Place the dough in a well-oiled bowl. Turn the dough in the bowl so that it becomes lightly filmed with the oil. Cover the bowl with a damp towel and place it to rise in the refrigerator.

Chilling and Rising

The rise in the refrigerator will be very slow. It will take the dough about 3 to 4 hours to rise to between 1½ and 1¾ times its original bulk. During this time the dough needs no attention; you are free to do as you please.

At the end of this 3- to 4-hour period, the dough should be thoroughly chilled. Take it out of the refrigerator for a moment and punch it down well. Make sure that every bit of air has been released from the dough. Return the dough to its oiled bowl (re-oil if necessary), turn it in the bowl, cover with the slightly damp towel, and refrigerate it again. At this point, the dough will be fairly dormant.

Resting the Dough

You are now going to allow the dough to rest in the refrigerator (it will also rise very slightly) for a minimum of 2 hours and a maximum of overnight, depending on your time schedule. You will *not* punch or knead the dough ever again in this recipe, because you do *not* want to activate the gluten any further. The gluten must be calm and quiet in order to roll the butter in properly. If the gluten is active, the dough will not roll out. After the dough has rested and you are ready to continue with the recipe, proceed with preparing the butter.

Preparing the Butter

Pound 3 sticks of cold, sweet butter with a rolling pin. This is to soften it. Knead in the remainder of the ½ cup flour. The butter is kneaded to make it approximately the same consistency as the dough; this way the butter and dough combine more easily. The butter must become malleable but remain cold. If you take too long and the butter warms up, refrigerate it for a few minutes. Form the butter into a 6-inch circle.

Knock the *unpunched*, cold dough out of its bowl and onto the floured cloth.

Roll out the *unpunched* dough into a circle that is about twice the size of the butter. Put the butter in the middle.

Wrap up the butter like a parcel. Seal edges well. Flour the parcel well. Turn it upsidedown. This will help to keep the seams closed while you roll.

REMINDER: Keep the rolling surface well floured at all times.

Now start the rolling and folding (turns). For croissants do only 4 turns. (Ordinary puff pastry requires 6 turns.)

Turns One and Two

Roll out the parcel into a long rectangle. Exact measurements are not important: 9 by 20 inches will work as well as 10 by 18 inches, etc. Do not roll over the edge of the dough that you are rolling toward, because this might cause the butter to pop through. Roll the dough in both directions — width as well as length — to create equal pressure on the butter inside the dough.

Fold top to bottom and then bottom to top. Turn the dough a quarter turn so that the open edge is to your right. Roll and fold again. Make 2 depressions with your fingers. This is customarily done in bakeries so that a new shift of bakers can tell how many turns the previous shift completed.

Flour the dough well, place it on a floured plate, cover it with plastic wrap, and refrigerate for 1 to 1½ hours.

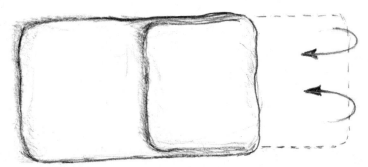

Turns Three and Four

With the open edge on your right roll the dough, fold it and turn a quarter turn. This is turn 3.

Again with the open edge on your right, roll the dough, fold it and turn a quarter turn. This is turn 4. (Make 4 depressions with your fingers.)

Flour the dough well, place it on a floured plate, cover it with plastic wrap, and refrigerate at least 2 hours or overnight, depending on the timetable you have chosen (see page 79).

Shaping the Croissants

Work with only enough dough for 4 croissants at a time; if you try larger amounts, the dough will become too soft to handle. Have 2 well-greased and floured jelly-roll pans ready.

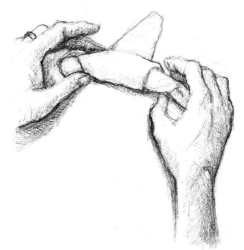

Take out the dough, pound it if it is hard, roll it out as if you are going to do a 5th turn, and cut it in half. Refrigerate half.

Roll out the remaining half to make it a few inches longer.

Cut it in 3 equal parts. Work with only 1 part at a time. Refrigerate the other parts. Roll out Part 1. Divide into 4 right triangles.

Roll out the point and roll out the base to make the triangle isosceles. Roll up the triangle starting from the base, and then bend the ends into a crescent shape.

Place the rolled croissant on the prepared jelly-roll pan. The point of the triangle should be underneath so that the croissant will not uncurl. Each dozen should take 15 minutes to shape.

The Last Rise

Cover the shaped croissants with a very slightly dampened, lightweight dish towel. If the towel is too damp, it will stick to the dough. (By far the easiest plan of action is to shape the croissants the night before you want them and to refrigerate them all night. There will be very little rising during the night. When you wake up in the morning, proceed with the room temperature rise as follows.) Allow yourself 2½ hours for the rise, to be on the safe side. At normal room temperature (70 to 75 degrees), the dough will rise in about an hour. On cold days, it will take longer; on hot days, less. However, if it is hot, you *must* alternate room temperature rising with refrigeration, otherwise the butter will leak out of the dough. In any case, after the shaped croissants are fully doubled in bulk, they should be refrigerated for at least 20 to 30 minutes (and a maximum of about 4 hours), to solidly chill the butter. This way you will get the full "bursting" potential from the butter when the croissants are placed in your very hot oven.

Glazing the Croissants

Ten to 15 minutes before baking, preheat your oven to 450 to 475 degrees. Use a pastry brush to glaze the fully risen croissants with an egg mixed with 2 tablespoons of water.

Baking the Croissants

Unless you have a large oven and can fit both baking sheets on the same shelf, bake only 1 dozen at a time. Refrigerate the second dozen while the first one bakes. Place the cookie sheet on the second level from the bottom in the hot oven. Bake the croissants for 5 minutes. Then lower the heat to 400 degrees and bake them about 10 to 15 minutes longer, or until they look beautifully browned. If necessary, place the baking sheet on a higher level for the last few minutes to brown the tops nicely. Then remove the croissants to a rack to cool for about 10 minutes before serving. Use a spatula. Remember to reheat your oven to 450 to 475 degrees before baking the second dozen.

If you plan to store the croissants, let them cool completely before wrapping and refrigerating or freezing. Always heat up stored croissants in a 350-degree oven for 8 to 10 minutes before serving.

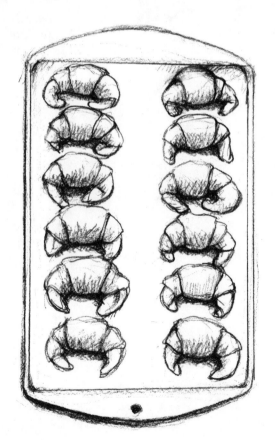

THREE TIMETABLES FOR MAKING CROISSANTS

	Complete in 1 day	Complete in 2 days	Complete in 3 days
Preparing basic dough	40 minutes-1 hour depending on skill (early in the morning)	DAY I 40 minutes-1 hour (early in the morning)	DAY I 40 minutes-1 hour (early evening)
The chilling (First rise in the refrigerator)	3-4 hours	3-4 hours	3-4 hours Finished later that first evening. Punch down, replace in refrigerator, and go to sleep. TOTAL DAY I: 4-5 hours
Resting in the refrigerator	2 hours	2 hours or longer. (You can proceed in 2 hours or leave dough refrigerated until evening.)	DAY II Overnight
Incorporating butter and turns 1 and 2; resting and chilling	10-15 minutes for incorporating butter and turns 1 and 2. Resting and chilling: 1-1½ hours.		
Turns 3 and 4; resting and chilling	Turns 3 and 4 take 5 minutes. Resting and chilling: 2 hours.	Turns 3 and 4 take 5 minutes. Rest and chill overnight. TOTAL DAY I: Morning: 4-4½ hours Evening: 1¾ hours	Turns 3 and 4 take 5 minutes. Rest and chill all day. Proceed with shaping late evening.
Shaping	30-45 minutes	DAY II 30-45 minutes	30-45 minutes. TOTAL DAY II: Morning: 1¾ hours Evening: 45 minutes
Final rise and chilling	2½ hours	2½ hours	DAY III 2½ hours
Baking	30 minutes	30 minutes TOTAL DAY II: 3½ hours	30 minutes TOTAL DAY III: 3 hours
	TOTAL HOURS: 12½-13½ hours		

Danish Pastry

Real Danish pastry, as it is made in Denmark, is made from croissant dough. Various fillings are wrapped in the butter-rich dough and formed into different shapes. Does this mean that the weary American traveler who casually stops at a diner for a Danish and coffee is actually getting such a sophisticated pastry? No! He is eating a piece of sweetened bread dough that is artificially colored to make it look eggy, and artificially flavored to make it taste buttery. The first time that you taste a real Danish, it is a revelation. This is one of the most sublime pastries that you can create.

The shape of the Danish is dependent on its type of filling. Danish pastries, as well as croissants, are baked in a very hot oven. If the filling is a very delicate one, such as the almond paste, it must be totally enclosed so that it will not get scorched. If the filling can take the heat, such as the brown sugar streusel, it can be exposed.

In this chapter there are instructions for five fillings and four shapes. Instructions for baking the pastries follow the last recipe, on page 84. One recipe of croissant dough will make 24 large Danish pastries or about 48 small ones. A good idea for a gala brunch is to make half the croissant dough into croissants and the other half into assorted Danish. Note that the shaping instructions give measurements for large Danish. To make the small size, simply cut the measurements in half.

1 recipe croissant dough

Handling the Dough

Prepare the dough exactly as the croissant recipe instructs. When you are ready to fill the Danish, grease 2 jelly roll-pans with solid vegetable shortening. Sprinkle a few tablespoons of flour into each pan and knock the flour about to make an even coating. Then knock out the excess. Chill the pans while filling the Danish. Divide the dough exactly as you would for the croissants: roll the dough out as if you were about to do a 5th turn, and cut the dough in half. Refrigerate half. Divide the remaining dough in thirds and refrigerate 2 parts. You are left with ⅙ of the dough, enough for 4 large or 8 petite Danish. Because the dough softens very quickly, you should not try to handle more than this at one time.

Be sure that your cloth and rolling pin are well floured at all times. The cut edges of the dough become very sticky. Frequently sprinkle flour on these edges as you form the Danish, and brush it off so that there are no floury clumps.

Danish Pockets

These square-shaped envelopes completely enclose the delicate fillings. Both are typical of the delectable pastries the Danes call Wienerbrød, *"Vienna bread."*

ALMOND PASTE FILLING

To fill 8 large or 16 small pastries

¼ cup sweet butter, softened to
   room temperature
¼ cup sugar
7-ounce package soft-style almond
   paste (Odense brand)
2 egg yolks
¼ teaspoon vanilla extract
⅜ teaspoon almond extract

Cream the butter and sugar together well, using a wooden spoon. Blend in the almond paste. Beat in the egg yolks and the vanilla and almond extracts. The mixture will be as soft as mashed potatoes, but it will harden when it is chilled. This filling may be made in advance and kept several days in the refrigerator.

CREAM CHEESE FILLING

To fill 6 large or 12 small pastries

8 ounces cream cheese, softened
   to room temperature
3 tablespoons honey
⅓-½ cup raisins

Cream the cheese and the honey together. As you fill each pastry, press the raisins into the cheese mixture. The cheese mixture may be prepared 1 or 2 days in advance and refrigerated.

Forming the Pockets

You are ready to work with one-sixth of the chilled dough, which will be in a strip approximately 3 by 9 inches.

Roll the dough out to make it a little bit wider. It will now be about 5 by 9 inches. Cut the dough into 4 rectangles. Roll 1 rectangle at a time into a square about 5 inches on each side. Turn the dough over on the cloth occasionally as you roll, to avoid sticking. Place a heaping tablespoon of filling in the center of the square. Fold 3 corners up over the filling. Brush the last corner with a little cold water and then fold it also over the top, pressing to make it adhere well. (The cold water will act like glue.) Place the finished pastries on the prepared, chilled baking sheets.

Streusel Snails

2 tablespoons sweet butter
¼ cup flour
¼ cup brown sugar
1 teaspoon cinnamon
Pinch of salt
¼-⅓ cup broken walnut meats

Combine the first 5 ingredients in a bowl and blend them together with your fingers or a wooden spoon. The streusel may be made in advance and refrigerated for 2 or 3 days.

Forming the Snails

You are ready to work with one-sixth of the chilled dough, which will be in a strip approximately 3 by 9 inches. Roll the dough into a rectangle about 6 by 9 inches. Turn the dough over occasionally while rolling, to cut down on the sticking. Sprinkle the streusel evenly on the dough, leaving a ¾-inch strip at the top of the dough empty. Be sure the streusel goes right to the edges on the other 3 sides, so that all the Danish will be evenly filled. Sprinkle the nuts over the streusel and press them in with your fingers. Brush the empty strip at the top with cold water.

Starting at the bottom end, roll up the dough like a jelly roll. Roll the dough tightly, because you do not want pockets of air inside the roll. Press the finished roll on the cloth for a moment, with the seam underneath, to make sure that it is well sealed. (It is the moistened empty edge of the dough that is actually holding the whole roll together.) Cut the roll in half, and then each half in 3. Place the snails cut side down on the cloth, and with a floured rolling pin, roll over them, 2 at a time, to flatten them slightly. Place the snails on the prepared, chilled baking sheets.

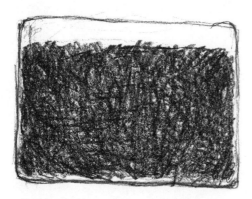

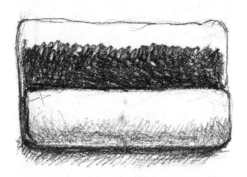

Prune Boats

1 cup dried prunes, canned moist-
  pack if available
2 tablespoons sugar
2 tablespoons apricot nectar, orange
  juice, or pineapple juice

Puree the prunes with the sugar and the juice in a food processor or an electric blender. If you cannot find the canned moist-dried prunes, use regular boxed prunes, but they will first have to be simmered in water to cover for about 20 minutes. Drain them and puree with 2 tablespoons of their cooking liquid or with one of the juices above. The amount of sugar needed will vary with the sweetness of the prunes. The finished puree should be pleasantly sweet, but not candylike.

Forming the Boats

You are ready to work with one-sixth of the chilled dough, which will be in a strip approximately 3 by 9 inches. Roll the dough out to make it a little bit wider, about 5 by 9 inches. Cut the dough into 4 rectangles. Roll 1 rectangle at a time into a square about 5 inches on each side. Turn the square so that it is facing you as a diamond. Place a heaping tablespoon of filling in the center and pull the righthand point over the filling. Lightly moisten the lefthand point with cold water and place it over the center, pressing to make it adhere well. To keep the 2 remaining points from baking too fast (the pastry here is thinner than in the center), fold them part way in. Use cold water to make them stick, if necessary. This way the prune filling will still show a little, but the pastry here has been doubled and it will all bake at the same rate. Place the boats on the prepared, chilled baking sheets.

Pains au Chocolat

This delightful treat should perhaps be in a category by itself, but I am including it here because it is made from filled croissant dough. Treat it exactly as you would the other Danish but omit glazing with apricot jam after baking.

For the filling you need 1 ounce of sweet or semi-sweet chocolate per pastry. Use an excellent quality of bar chocolate that you can cut or break into 1-ounce strips measuring about ¾ by 3 inches.

Forming the Pains

You are ready to work with one-sixth of the chilled dough, which will be in a strip approximately 3 by 9 inches. Roll the dough out to make it a little bit wider. It will now be about 5 by 9 inches. Cut the dough into 4 rectangles. Roll 1 rectangle at a time into a square about 5 inches on each side. Turn the dough over on the cloth occasionally as you roll, to avoid sticking.

Arrange the stick of chocolate toward the right side of the square. Fold the dough over the top and bottom ends of the stick. Moisten the lefthand edge of the dough. Starting on the right, roll up the dough into a flat cigar shape. Press the finished cigar, seam side down, on the cloth for a moment, to make sure that it is well sealed. This will also flatten out the pastry a bit. Place the finished *pains* on the prepared, chilled baking sheets.

The Last Rise, Glazing with Egg Before Baking, and Baking the Danish

The instructions for these procedures in the croissant section on pages 77-78 are exactly the same for the Danish. In fact, if your oven is big enough to accommodate 2 baking sheets on the same shelf, you can bake Danish and croissants at the same time. For the large Danish, you may find that the baking time needs to be extended by 4 to 5 minutes, so that they brown nicely.

Glazing the Baked Danish

When you remove the Danish from the oven, place them immediately on wire racks to cool. While they are still hot, glaze them with apricot jam that has been melted with a little water (¼ cup jam and 1 tablespoon water). Use a pastry brush to apply the glaze. Let the Danish cool 20 to 30 minutes before serving. (The enclosed fillings become terribly hot in the oven; you do not want to burn your guests!)